Observing Children and Young People

4th Edition

Also available from Continuum

Good Practice in the Early Years – Janet Kay
Protecting Children – Janet Kay
Teaching 3–8 – Mark O'Hara
Childminder's Handbook – Allison Lee

Observing Children and Young People

4th Edition

Carole Sharman,
Wendy Cross
and Diana Vennis

continuum

Continuum International Publishing Group

The Tower Building   80 Maiden Lane, Suite 704

11 York Road   New York, NY 10038

London SE1 7NX

www.continuumbooks.com

First published by Cassell 1995
Reprinted 1996

Second edition published by Continuum 2000
Third edition 2004
Reprinted 2004, 2005 and 2006

British Library Cataloguing-in-Publication Data
A catalogue record for this book is available from the British Library.

ISBN: 0826492738 (paperback)
      780826492739 (paperback)

Library of Congress Cataloging-in-Publication Data
A catalog record for this book is available from the Library of Congress.

Typeset by Ben Cracknell Studios | www.benstudios.co.uk
Printed and bound in Great Britain by Ashford Colour Press Ltd, Gosport, Hampshire

Contents

Preface

This book is intended for use by anyone working with children and young people aged from birth to 16 years. Its main aim is to encourage childcare practitioners, playworkers and educators to enhance their experience of observing, in order that they can recognize children's and young people's skills and abilities and identify their needs. This will make planning for their future development much more specific to the individual need.

The book is not linked specifically to any course of study or area of work but, where practical, links are made to early learning goals of the foundation stage when discussing areas of development. There are also links to the occupational standards written for NVQs in Children's Care, Learning and Development, and in Playwork. Other courses of study that might benefit from the book include the Certificate and Diploma in Childcare and Education, the Certificate and Diploma in Early Years Practice, and Teaching Assistant and Home-based Childcare qualifications. These qualifications all have an element requiring observation to support the study of children's development and planning for relevant activities. Anyone studying for foundation degrees in Early Childhood Studies, Early Years or similar could also benefit as the evaluations have been extended for some of the observations to include more emphasis on linking development to theorists.

By presenting evidence in the format of an observation, whether as part of course work or your workplace recording system, you will be demonstrating a detailed knowledge of development and the principles underlying different types of observation. You should also be considering their strengths, weaknesses and possible bias as a method of recording.

How to use this book

The book is intended as a source of reference that can be dipped into throughout your training and beyond. However, if you have never done observations, or are unsure how to begin, you might want to go through the book in the order it is written. The chapters have been designed to lead you through the process, building on knowledge gained earlier. The observations are highlighted for ease of reference and there are specific activities for you to complete in order to help build up your expertise.

This book references the National Curriculum of England and Wales. It is hoped that readers in other countries will benefit from the general guidance on how to carry out observations, and how these can be linked to their own curriculum.

Acknowledgements

The authors would like to thank the Early Years students from Highbury, Godalming and Norland Colleges for their ideas. They would also like to thank the nursery and primary schools in the Portsmouth area, Early Learners Streatham and Crofton Ann Dale School, Stubbington, who allowed us to observe and photograph their children. Thanks also to the parents for their permission to use the photographs.

All photographs are by Carole Sharman.

Summaries of Early Learning Goals are reproduced with the permission of QCA.

Introduction

Watching and listening to their children is a favourite pastime for parents. Some say they 'waste' half a day marvelling at what their young babies can do.

As future carers and educators of children and young people, you are probably aware that it is not a waste of time to observe progress and behaviour. This is how you learn what stage of development they have reached. Observation will enable you to compare their progress with the expected range for the age group, and to plan activities and support techniques that will lead them forward to the next stage. This could be the physical abilities of toddlers or the social skills demonstrated by young teenagers. Observation will alert you to the needs of the child or adolescent who has not reached the expected 'norm', or is far ahead of it, so that you can monitor the situation and request the appropriate professional help if required. It will allow you to enjoy each individual's unique qualities.

One way of monitoring progress would be to study the stages of development, Key Stages and SATs attainment for the age group, and then spend your entire time watching and listening to see if they have reached the required level. This is obviously neither practical nor desirable in the work situation. As professional carers and educators you will, with practice, be alerted to children's and young people's behaviour and attainment that gives cause for concern. As learners (or even experienced practitioners) in the field you need to be equipped with the tools to enable you to make those judgements in an informed way.

The most appropriate way to monitor progress, and compare it with what you are learning, or know, about the way children and young people mature and develop, is to undertake *observations*. The main aim of this book is to lead you through the process, and give you confidence to be a skilled practitioner.

Chapter 1 discusses in more detail the reasons why we do observations, and some of the methods that can be used to record them. It is related mainly to the younger age groups but also considers why we may want to carry out observations with the over-8s. It encourages you to think about children's different needs and experiences. The 'Skills you may observe' section (p. 12) considers the skills you may observe, as one of the main functions of the book is to emphasize the positive aspects of doing observations.

Chapter 2 takes you through the stages for recording the written/narrative form of observation and gives you opportunities to try things for yourself. Chapter 3 gives a more comprehensive guide to the various methods with examples of each, followed by some Aims and Objectives for you to decide on the most appropriate format for recording. These now include some reasons why you might want to carry out observations on older age groups. Chapter 4 reviews the benefits of recording observations in more detail, and discusses why observations are important for the children or young adults in your care. In Chapter 5 the ability to link observations to Early Learning Goals (ELGs) or Key Stage Assessment is developed. Chapter 6 is divided into developmental areas for the younger age groups (0 to 8), with suggestions for activities that can be related to the criteria for ELGs. This should help you with ideas for extending children's experiences. It also discusses the importance of observations when working with special needs children. Because of the very structured nature of the school curriculum, suggestions for older children are limited to ideas for 'out of school' activities. Chapter 7 provides a summary of developmental stages that you can refer to; but remember that children will come to you with very different social and cultural experiences which may influence their development. Chapter 7 offers guidelines only.

Observations are part of the curriculum for all childcare and education courses. They provide evidence for the portfolios of candidates undertaking NVQs in Children's Care, Learning and Development. They are often viewed with some dismay. The second aim of this book is to make you aware of their value: the difference that observations can make to your work practice; and that they can be interesting and fun to do.

Look at the picture below and think about what it tells you. Read the book and carry out the activities and then look at the picture again. You should understand a lot more about the learning taking place.

Figure I.1 A typical nursery classroom

CHAPTER ONE

Why Do Observations?

At the end of this chapter you will be able to answer the following:

- **Why do we observe children?**

- **How can we observe them?**

'Observations are boring.'

'I can do the observation, but I never know what to say in the comments.'

'I find it very difficult to know what to write.'

'It is very hard to watch the children and write at the same time.'

'Why do we have to do observations?'

Above are some of the comments made by students when asked what they thought of having to do child observations. Below are some of the comments made by parents about their children:

'I wonder why he did that?'

'Why can't she understand what I want her to do?'

'He is very naughty, he can't share his toys.'

'She doesn't like to be left for a moment – it is so frustrating.'

'He wants to feed himself, but makes such a mess that I can't let him.'

Practitioners and parents can both learn more about why and when children and young people do something by having knowledge of development, and by observing what they do. Without that knowledge we can misunderstand what they are trying to tell us and this can make life difficult for everyone.

All children and young people develop at their own speed. There are genetic and environmental influences that can affect the rate at which they develop, but broadly they will follow the same sequence. The way that children and young people develop has been studied by many researchers and their results published in the textbooks you will be using in your studies. Most research requires observation. For instance Green (2004) states:

> Researchers throughout the health and social care sector may use observations as primary research to gain information within child and young adult settings.

One of the main reasons we observe is to see if the children and young adults in our care are following the general pattern. Observation is an important tool for you to see in practice what you have learned in theory.

Direct observation as an assessment method has four determining features:

> Behaviour is observed in a natural setting.
>
> Behaviour is recorded or coded as it occurs.
>
> Impartial, objective observers record behaviour.
>
> Behaviour is described in clear, crisp terms, requiring little or no inference by the observer. (Ramsay et al., 2002)

The authors do stress, however, that observers should be as unobtrusive as possible so as not to disrupt or alter behaviour, and that where possible observations should take place in multiple settings in order to see if behaviour is more likely to occur under certain conditions.

As well as using observations to discover how children and young people are developing and behaving, we can also make use of observations to plan areas for play and learning. This can be very useful for practitioners in the playwork field.

> Playworkers exist to support children's natural play and they do this by creating spaces where play can happen. Then they unobtrusively observe, intervene very occasionally, and then reflect on what they have seen and done. (CACHE, 2005)

Cache (2005) also states that:

> Observations are necessary when they need to plan play spaces (PW9.2), support self-directed play (PW9.3) and help children and young people manage risk during play (PW9.4).

Activity

Without turning back to the Introduction, note down your answers to the following questions:

1 Why do we observe children and young people?

2 What can we see?

3 What can we learn by observing them?

4 How can we help them by carrying out our observations?

We will discuss these questions at the end of the chapter and you can compare your answers with the suggestions given.

Having decided that observation is a tool that can help with your understanding, and benefit the children and young people in your care, we need to look at the best ways of carrying out the observations and recording the results.

Here are two important points to consider before proceeding:

1 An observation is like a camera shot, and although it is said that the camera does not lie, it may distort. We should not make judgements about children and young people based upon a single observation. We may be alerted to a problem, but need to follow it up in order to reach an informed conclusion.

2 The very fact that we are carrying out the observation can make a difference to the way that the child or young person behaves. They may become inhibited or embarrassed, or may play to the audience. Try an experiment: take a camera and a tape recorder into the workplace and see the response when you try to record the 'normal' routine.

If you remember these points then you will be able to make the best use of your observations and also decide which is the best method to use. Researchers will often use video to record children's behaviour so that they can play it back numerous times in order to see in detail the responses. This is particularly true when observing babies, and you have undoubtedly seen the results on television. You may be able to do this, but we are concentrating on the more usual methods of written evidence. The method you choose will normally be dependent on the timescale and what you are hoping to discover.

In the following pages we discuss:

- **Observation methods**

- **Children's and young people's needs and experiences**

- **Skills you may observe.**

Observation Methods

Observations can be carried out in many formats, and the examples given here are meant to give you an idea of how some of them can be recorded. We will be discussing all the methods you can employ, their best uses and the exact way to lay out observations in the following chapters.

1. Narrative/free description

This is the style of observation that you will probably start with. It involves watching a child or group of children and noting down what you see. You will need to sit quietly and try to draw as little attention to yourself as possible, remembering that your interaction with the children can affect their behaviour. One way to deter children from talking to you is to avoid eye contact. If they become aware that you are writing, you might say that you are doing some college work.

Written observations usually cover a short period of time. They should be written in the present tense because you are recording things as they happen. Although you will need to set the scene by describing what is going on around, you need to remember that your main focus is the child you are observing.

An example of how you might write is shown below.

Observation

Setting The home corner in a reception class.

Carl puts on a white gown and a pair of rabbit's ears then starts hopping about. John sits down beside the telephone and then gets up and walks over to the cupboard. He takes out two bowls and puts them onto the floor, then walks over and picks up Carl. He carries Carl over to the bowls and sets him down.

'Eat up, rabbit.'

Carl kneels down and pretends to eat the food. John starts to make 'brrr brrr' noises. He goes over to the telephone, picks it up and listens.

'Auntie is coming to see us.'

Carl appears not to have heard but after a minute he gets up and walks over to the dressing-up box.

He takes out a skirt which he puts on over the rabbit outfit. He walks over to John and in a high squeaky voice says: 'Hello, I've come for a visit.'

John looks at Carl and then walks out of the home corner over to the craft table.

2. Checklists/pre-coded categories

Checklists can be used to record the activities of a single child or a group of children. Unlike the written/narrative observation, which only requires you to write a record of what you see, a checklist needs to be prepared in advance. You will need to consider what you want to find out about the children. Checklist observations are regularly used in schools to record the progress of children. It is important for the teacher to be aware of the needs of the individual child so that programmes can be developed. Most modern classrooms allow the children a certain amount of freedom to decide their own learning activities so it is essential to keep a record of their achievements. It is important to note here that we are recording a child's *achievements*, not their failure to do something. Of course we may identify a *need* while we are doing so.

An example of a checklist for your group in nursery is shown in Figure 1.1.

N.B. The children may not complete this on one day or in the order given. That does not matter. Also the younger the child, the less likely they are to 'perform to order'. You may obtain a truer picture if you make the assessment into a game.

Figure 1.1 Example of checklist

Activity	Sam	Liam	Susan	Shanaz	William
Stands on one leg for three seconds	✓	✓	✓	✓	✗
Jumps in place	✓	✓	✓	✓	✓
Hops on one foot	✗	✗	✓	✗	✓
Kicks ball	✓	✓	✓	✓	✓
Catches large ball	✗	✓	✗	✓	✓
Pedals tricycle	✓	✓	✓	✓	✓

3. Time sampling/structured description

As the name suggests, this form of recording consists of a series of written records at intervals throughout a period of time. The length of time between the observations, and the length of time you observe for, will depend on the overall timescale for the completed record. This will normally be decided by the reason you are carrying out the observation in the first place. For example, if you want to discover whether a child is able to concentrate for the duration of a storytime you might decide to look at that child every minute and record what they are doing. It might look something like this:

Observation

10.01 a.m. Sitting quietly looking at the teacher.

10.02 a.m. Concentrating on the picture being shown to the group.

10.03 a.m. Pulling up her socks and carefully turning over the tops.

10.04 a.m. Responds to her name being called by the teacher.

10.05 a.m. Has her hand up to answer a question which is asked about the story.
. . . and so on.

If a child was aggressive or did not appear to mix very well you might want to observe that child for a morning or even a whole day. In that instance you would probably decide to make the interval 20 minutes or half an hour. Your observation might look something like this:

Observation

9.00 a.m. Comes into class and looks back at mother in the doorway. Spoken to by the class teacher and comes and sits on the floor. Spoken to by another child but does not respond.

9.30 a.m. Working with a group of six children doing number activities. Asked to pass the pencil container by one of the children - does not respond. Asked again in a louder voice - pushes the container across table but does not make any eye contact.

10.00 a.m. Painting a picture beside another child. Looks across at the other's drawing and stands slightly closer. Approached by teacher.

'What an interesting picture - would you like to tell me what it is?'

Smiles but does not answer.

'Is it a bus?'

Child nods but does not speak.

10.30 a.m. Standing beside the wall in the playground. Moves and goes to stand near the playground duty teacher but does not say anything. Kicks a ball that comes close and walks after it. 'Do you want to play?' asks the child.

Nods and joins in the game, but no speech heard.

. . . and so on.

Figure 1.2 Tracking observation

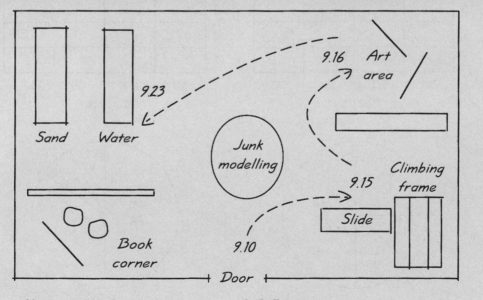

Key – – → Route taken   9.15 Time left area

4. Tracking/structured description

A tracking observation involves following a child for a length of time to discover where they go and what they do. This could be recorded as a written observation but an alternative is to show the result in the form of a diagram. It requires you to draw out the area in which the child will be working in advance. This might be the nursery, classroom or outdoor play area. The most obvious use would be to record the activities of a child in the free play time. It would enable you to see if they stay with one activity or flits from one to another. You could also use this method to record the number of social contacts a child makes in a given time.

The observation might look like that shown in Figure 1.2.

Figure 1.3 Recording results in bar charts and pie charts

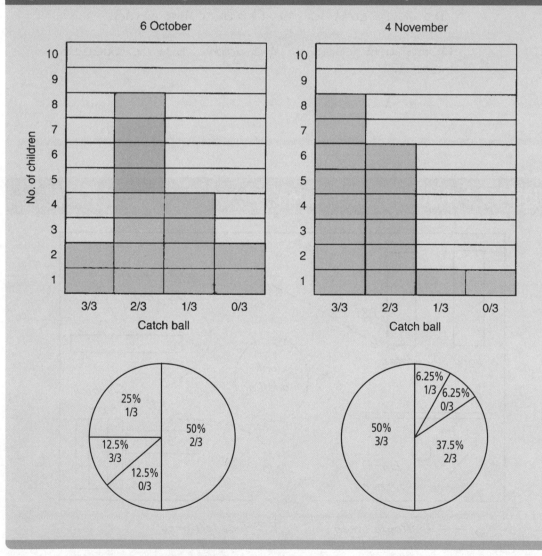

5. Pie and bar charts/structured description

Pie and bar charts are a useful pictorial way of recording the results of an observation of the whole class. You might want to discover how many children could manage a physical skill like ball catching. You could set up an activity where you threw a ball to the children from a distance of 5 feet. Your record would show how many children caught the ball three times out of three; two times out of three; once out of three; and not at all. If your result showed the children had some difficulty with this you might then introduce some activities which give practice in the skill and then repeat the observation. Figure 1.3 on p. 8 shows what the results might look like.

These methods have many uses for collecting information about the children, but they can also be used to give objective evidence about the equipment used in the nursery/classroom/adventure playground, etc. You can watch areas of the setting and note how many times an item is used, e.g. number table, computer, climbing frame. This could give you an opportunity to look at how you would arrange things in the future – or where you might station yourself to give added interest!

Understanding Children's and Young People's Needs and Experiences

We have discussed various ways of carrying out observations and later we will return to them in more detail. One of the reasons identified for doing observations was 'to meet the *needs* of the children'. Children and young people are unique and to be aware of their qualities we need to:

- Take an interest in what they are doing.

- Listen to what they are saying.

- Learn from what they are telling us.

Children and young people may communicate their needs in a variety of individual ways. Older children may be able to tell you what they want, but could also behave in a way that suggests there is a need for support. Younger children usually demonstrate their need using more primitive methods. For instance, one child may scream for attention while a second bites another person to express their need. Both these behaviours are essentially anti-social but we might understand the reasons if we observe why it is happening.

Observation

Adam (20 months) is playing with a ball in the garden. He throws it into the air and then tries to kick it. He moves the ball by walking into it. When it rolls under the chair he chuckles with delight and shouts 'Goal!'

Two older children (3 and 4 years) come out of the house to watch. When the ball comes near they pick it up and start to throw it to each other. Adam stands and watches and waits for his turn but they do not include him in the game. The ball rolls towards Adam and he picks it up and hugs it to himself. The 4-year-old walks over and takes it out of Adam's hand and kicks it to the other child. Adam tries to get the ball again but the 3-year-old picks it up, laughs and holds it above her head. As she lowers her arms Adam runs over and bites her hand. She screams and the adults run out to see what has happened. Adam just stands looking bewildered.

'You naughty boy,' says his mother.

Take the example of biting – the observation above could help sort out the problem.

Adam will have to learn that it is not a good thing to bite, but he also needs to have someone who will try to understand his problems before he is able to put them into words.

Children always want you to see what they can see, watch with them and enjoy experiences together. A child's excitement is intense when they shout 'Look at me'. If you observe children while they are working instead of just admiring the end product you may be surprised at their abilities. For example, a child presents a soggy brown painting to be put in the drying rack. The nursery nurse says: 'I hope it will be dry by going home time.'

When presented with the painting the mother says: 'Very nice dear, what else have you done this morning?'

The following record of an observation demonstrates what the picture was meant to be.

Observation

Dionne (4 years 1 month) puts on an apron and walks over to the painting easel. She picks up the brush from the brown paint pot and draws a circle. She puts two blobs of paint in the circle and returns the brush to the pot. She takes the red brush and paints a curved line at the top of the paper and then puts a line of green below it. She smiles and says: 'A rainbow'.

She stands back for a moment then takes out the yellow brush and draws a sun next to the rainbow.

'Now we need rain.'

[She paints blobs of brown paint onto the picture.]

'It's raining very hard - here's a puddle.'

[She begins to paint lines of brown all over the picture.]

'It's pouring - Grandma is getting very wet.'

[Dionne stands back and looked at the brown picture.]

'I've finished.'

Children are very proud of their achievements, but you must remember that their ability to do something will depend on the amount of practice they have had. We may be tempted to make a judgement quickly from our observation of a child and question their level of development. We must remember *to take into account past experience and environment* before making any assumptions.

If we take the example of riding a bike, for instance, Mary Sheridan (1980) reports: Age 3 years – 'rides tricycle, using pedals, and can steer it round wide corners'.

If a child has a tricycle or attends playschool then that is probably true, but some will not have had that experience. If a child appears to have a delay in any developmental area we should provide activities which enable them to practise the skill before 'testing' their ability.

No one would expect you to take a driving test without having lessons – whatever your age.

To summarize then: *Children need adults to notice their achievements and provide an environment to support their further development.* This can be done by observing a child's progress and assessing their needs in all areas.

Figure 1.4 gives some examples of the ways adults can encourage children in their development. You will notice that the areas are linked together as it is inevitable that while you are providing for one, you will also be covering the others. Any activity is likely to include language and hopefully also build self-esteem.

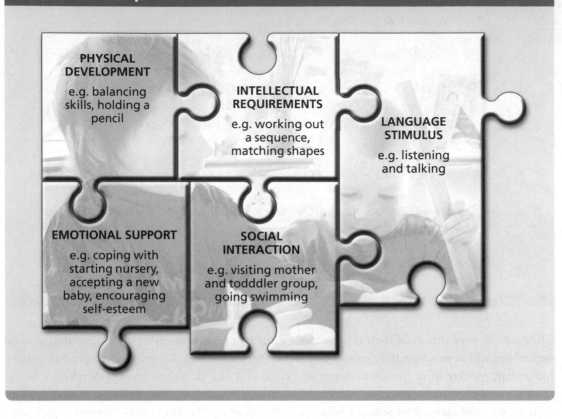

Figure 1.4 Examples of ways adults can encourage children in their development.

PHYSICAL DEVELOPMENT

e.g. balancing skills, holding a pencil

INTELLECTUAL REQUIREMENTS

e.g. working out a sequence, matching shapes

LANGUAGE STIMULUS

e.g. listening and talking

EMOTIONAL SUPPORT

e.g. coping with starting nursery, accepting a new baby, encouraging self-esteem

SOCIAL INTERACTION

e.g. visiting mother and todddler group, going swimming

Skills You May Observe

Children need to develop a variety of skills to enable them to fulfil their individual potential. As part of your observations you will need to identify the stage the child has reached so that you can provide experiences to encourage progress. An area that students often find difficult to define is *cognitive* or *intellectual*. Figure 1.5 shows some of the skills involved in the process of learning language and reasoning.

Memory and reasoning allow us to make educated guesses about things we have not directly experienced. The older the child the more they are able to do this. Younger children need to be able to see the problem in order to work it out. This is very obvious when working with numbers – young children need counters or fingers to find the answer but older ones are able to 'do it in their heads'. If you are aware of where the child has reached in their development by observing their skills you will be able to provide activities which will enable them to progress.

Figure 1.5 Some of the skills involved in memory, reasoning and language

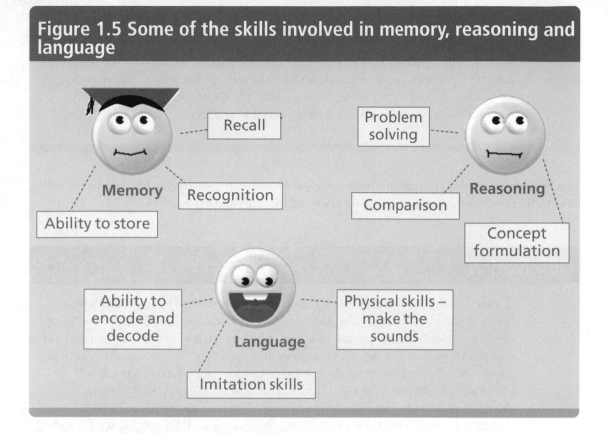

Observations linked with progress in skills

Let us consider a child's ability to complete a three-piece jigsaw. Skills developing are:

Physical   Intellectual fine manipulative skills, eye–hand co-ordination.
Intellectual problem solving, concentration, memory, concept of size–shape–colour.
Emotional   patience/control, frustration/satisfaction.
Social   sharing (with adult or child).
Language   association – pictures and words, new words/subjects.

Activity

Try to undertake the following: an observation of a 2-, 3- and 4-year-old each completing the same jigsaws.

1   **Make a comparison between the abilities of each child.**

2   **Notice the variation of levels of skills.**

3   **From your observations devise an action plan to increase the development of skills.**

Observation

For example, Philip (3) can complete a simple three-piece jigsaw. He now insists on placing the pieces upside down on the tray. He is obviously trying to find new ways of playing with them.

This is where your role as a facilitator becomes apparent. You can now develop his skills by providing newer/different/more complicated jigsaws to extend his skills and experiences.

Observation

Claire (2) cannot yet complete the jigsaw unaided. She needs an adult beside her to help. She picks up the pieces and puts them at random into the holes - pushing hard to fit them in. When they won't go in she gets frustrated, screws up her face and pushes harder then looks to the adult for help. Adult places hand on top of Claire's and guides the piece into the right place, allowing Claire the final feel of satisfaction when the piece drops into place. She persists in trying again - and each time with the help and patience of an adult she succeeds.

By observing the child and seeing the absorption in the activity you can tell that, although she cannot complete it without help, it is not so difficult that she will not develop the required skills to gain eventual success.

SUMMARY

You have now looked at various observation methods, thought about children's and young people's needs, and considered some of the skills you may require to encourage and develop them.

Before we move on to the next chapter, we need to look again at the questions posed at the beginning of this chapter and consider some of the answers you may have given. These might include:

1 Why do we observe children and young people? – to discover their unique qualities and talents.

2 What can we see? – what children and young people can do; how they approach problems and how they attempt to solve them; how they make use of space and facilities; children and youngsters enjoying themselves.

3 What can we learn by observing them? – what level they have reached; a better understanding of why a child or young person has done something; it will reinforce our knowledge of child development and allow us to reflect upon our practice; it helps us try to see things from the child's or young person's point of view.

4 How can we help them by carrying out our observation? – by providing activities, resources and support to facilitate their developing skills.

BY WATCHING CHILDREN AND YOUNG PEOPLE:

WE EVALUATE THEIR NEEDS

EXTEND THEIR EXPERIENCES

FACILITATE THEIR LEARNING.

REFERENCES

CACHE (Council for Awards in Child Health and Education) (2005) Handbook *Level 3 NVQ in Playwork*.

Green, S. (2004) *Research Methods in Health, Social and Early Years Care*. Cheltenham: Stanley Thorne.

Ramsay, M.C., Reynolds, C.R. and Kamphaus, R.W. (2002) *Essentials of Behavioral Assessment*. New York: John Wiley & Sons.

Sheridan, M. (1980) *From Birth to Five Years*. London: NFER.

CHAPTER TWO

A Step-by-step Guide to Presenting an Observation

Using the written/narrative style as an example

At the end of this chapter you will be able to answer the following:

- **Identify Aims and Objectives.**
- **Record detailed observations.**
- **Relate your findings to work practice.**

In the previous chapter we outlined some of the usual ways in which observations can be recorded. Now it is your turn to try out the skill. We will begin by looking in detail at how to organize and present an observation using the written/narrative format.

To help you through the stages that will follow we have started with an example of how a completed observation will look, with explanations for the headings used. The headings in bold blue type will actually always remain the same whichever format you use. An explanation of the headings is given in italic black type.

Observation

Observation no. 1   *It is important to number the observations so that you can refer to a particular example if you want to use it as NVQ evidence. It will also demonstrate your progress in an observation file.*

Date   23.6.2006 *There are two reasons for recording the date: (1) You may wish to repeat an observation at a later date in order to compare a child's ability with their previous performance; (2) It will enable you to work out the exact age of the child so that you can evaluate your results against the expected developmental stage.*

Time commenced   10.20 a.m.

Time completed 10.30 a.m. *This allows you to comment more easily on the length of time a child spent on an activity.*

Number of adults 1.

Number of children 4. *Although you may have decided to observe one child, it is useful to record the number of children in the group as this may have an influence on the behaviour.*

Name of child Manju. *It is only necessary to record the first, or a fictitious, name so that the record remains confidential if you are using the observation for study purposes.*

Age 3 years 10 months. *You will need to know the child's date of birth to work this out. It is important to record the exact age in years and months in order to make a fair comparison with developmental stages.*

Setting *The junk modelling table in the creative area of a nursery school. The children have a free choice of materials but a nursery nurse is available to offer advice if required. It is not necessary to identify the place by name (in order to maintain confidentiality), but it is useful to record the general background to the observation. It is also important to record if an adult is involved, as this is likely to affect the way the children behave.*

Aim *To observe a child who is nearly 4 years old during a junk modelling session in order to identify fine manipulative skills and problem-solving ability. The Aim of an observation should set out the broad areas of development that you wish to find out.*

Objectives *To observe and record Manju's ability to use scissors and glue spreader. To observe and record Manju's ability to plan her model and work out how to make it. The Objectives should identify the specific abilities that you wish to observe.*

Record of observation

Manju puts on an apron and approaches the table. She picks up a circular box and turns it over in her hands then puts it back down. She walks round to the other side of the table and selects a larger cereal packet then returns to her original place. She looks at the nursery nurse and smiles.

'What are you going to make?' asks the nursery nurse.

Manju looks at the display on the wall and says: 'A rocket'. She picks up some silver foil and carefully tears it in half. With a well-developed pincer grasp she picks up a glue spreader and dips it into the pot of glue. Some of the glue drips onto the newspaper covering the table as Manju carries the spreader over to her box. The nursery nurse moves the glue pot closer to Manju. Manju tips the glue off her spreader onto the box and smears it over half of one side, then she leans over and puts some more glue onto the spreader and places it on the box. Concentrating very hard, she uses the spreader to cover the whole side. She smiles as she continues to make patterns in the glue.

'Are you going to stick your silver paper on?' asks the nursery nurse.

Manju picks up a piece of the silver paper with her left hand and leans over to put some more glue on the spreader. She holds the paper in the palm of her hand and covers it with glue.

'I think you have enough glue now,' says the nursery nurse.

Manju places the piece of glue-covered silver paper onto the box. Her fingers stick to the paper, which lifts off as she attempts to fix it to the box. She looks across at the nursery nurse, who comes over to assist.

'I think you can put the other piece of paper on without any more glue.'

Manju selects a cardboard tube instead. She pushes it against the box and holds it in position for a few moments. When she moves her hand the tube falls off. She picks up the spreader and puts some glue around the end then pushes it down on the box again. As she lets go it falls over.

The nursery nurse picks up another piece of cardboard tube:

'Shall I show you how to fix it?'

Manju nods and watches as the nursery nurse makes a cut about 2 cm long down the side.

'Can you make some more cuts round the edge?'

The nursery nurse hands the scissors to Manju. She manages to put her fingers in them correctly and, holding the tube close to her body, she makes a short cut. She pulls the scissors out and attempts a second incision. The scissors come together at an angle but do not cut.

Manju begins to look anxious. The nursery nurse comes round the table and puts her hand over the scissors to guide them. Together they make several more cuts. The nursery nurse shows Manju how to bend the card back to make a bigger area to glue.

'Now you can stick it to your rocket.'

Manju spreads some glue onto the box and then puts the tube in place. She moves her hand and smiles when it stays in position.

'Do you want to add any more?' asks the nursery nurse.

Manju looks at the model and says: 'No'.

'Shall we put your rocket somewhere safe to dry?'

Manju nods then goes off to wash her hands.

The record should be written as it happens whenever possible. You should concentrate on the areas you are interested in as it will not be possible to record everything the child does.

Conclusion

Manju decided what she wanted to make before she started the model by observing what was on the wall frieze in the creative area. She was able to use the glue spreader and enjoyed putting lots of glue onto the box. She used more than was necessary to stick the paper to it and spent some time making patterns which she appeared to enjoy.

Manju had some difficulty using the scissors but she held them properly. She was not yet able to work out how to fix the cardboard tube to the box, but managed to complete her rocket with the assistance of the nursery nurse.

The conclusion should summarize what you observed and match it to what you hoped to find out – your Objectives.

Evaluation

The developmental milestones for the 4-year-old (p. 160) state that they are 'able to use scissors with practice', and are 'beginning to name drawings before starting'. Manju is not quite 4, but she held the scissors properly and made a partially successful attempt to cut the tube, which is a difficult shape. She was able to name what she planned to do before starting. Manju appears to be operating well within the normal limits.

The evaluation should compare your findings with what you expect children and young people to be able to do at that age. You should use a recognized source in order to make your comparison. Examples could be the milestones in Chapter 7, foundation stage stepping stones or Key Stage targets. You can also compare the child with other children in the class who are the same age. Where possible you should also use current research or theorists.

Recommendations

Continue to offer opportunities for planning her own activities. Encourage activities that will help to strengthen finger muscles (fine manipulative skills), e.g. Play-doh, construction toys.

One of the main uses for your observations is to enable you to plan activities that will help the children and young people perfect their skills and move forward. By observing what the child is doing you can organize suitable activities. This is backed up by the research of Lev Vygotsky, who concluded that children can learn more by the right amount of adult intervention. He used the term 'Zone of Proximal Development' to explain the range of potential for learning each person has compared to the learning that actually takes place in their environment.

Zone of Proximal Development: the distance between the actual development level as determined by independent problem solving and the level of potential development as determined through problem solving under adult guidance or in collaboration with more capable peers. (Vygotsky, 1978)

Now that you have seen how a completed observation is set out you should be ready to try the skill for yourself. The following sections have been arranged so that you can work your way through the activities and build on your knowledge.

Activity

1 **Discuss with your supervisor or work colleagues the need to undertake an observation. Then decide on a time when you are likely to be interrupted as little as possible.**

2 **Identify the child that you would like to observe and discuss with your supervisor how you will obtain parental permission. The nursery or school will have permission to keep records of observations undertaken for the child's personal file – but this is unlikely to cover observations that will be taken out of the establishment and seen by other professionals. All information is likely to come under the Data Protection Act so needs to be time constrained. Children are also protected by the Children Act and Human Rights Act. Parents have the right to know that you will respect their child's right to confidentiality.**

A possible template for your letter could be:

Dear Parent

I am currently studying for .... Part of the course requires me to complete observations to help me understand how children develop and learn. I am writing to ask permission to observe your child as part of this study, while [he/she] is in the nursery/school.

My observations will be undertaken during the normal nursery/school routine and will not interfere with [his/her] work and learning opportunities.

In line with Data Protection I anticipate that I will be retaining the data until ....

The observation findings will be seen by my supervisor, assessor, verifier/moderator and possibly by the external award verifier/moderator.

In order to maintain confidentiality I will use pseudonyms throughout – including name of establishment and child.

I would be very happy to share the finding with you.

3 **Sit quietly and record what the child does for five minutes.**

4 **When you have finished the observation, read it back to yourself.**

You may have found the above activity difficult. It is not easy to record what is taking place as you are trying to watch everything that is happening around you. While you are writing you may miss an important interaction. One way you can speed up your note taking, so that you do not need to have your head down all the time, is to develop a code. This can be quite simple. For example, you may put A→B. This could mean that child A (Ben) went up to child B (Sunil) and exchanged information. This might be very useful if you were recording a child's ability to socialize. You will need to think about possible shortcuts and then note them down, because it is not much use having a lot of observations that you are unable to read back.

This raises another important point about writing up your observations. THE SOONER YOU READ THEM THROUGH AND WRITE THEM OUT FULLY – THE EASIER IT WILL BE. A common excuse made by students who have failed to produce observations for marking is that they have lots 'in rough'. They then have great difficulty in remembering what some of the hasty scribble means. If you write up the observation while it is fresh in your mind you will often be able to visualize the situation again and know what you have written. Ten minutes of your lunch break used in this way can save you a lot of time later on.

Another way to make your recording easier is to identify clearly the reason why you are observing the child and what you hope to find out. This will give you your *Aims* and *Objectives*.

Activity

Figure 2.1 is a picture of two 4-year-olds playing in a sand tray, followed by an account of what took place during a 15-minute observation. (The sand had birdseed mixed in with it.) *Read through* the observation and then *make a list* of what you think it tells you about the children.

Figure 2.1 Two 4-year-olds playing in the sand

Observation

The children are standing either side of the sand tray running their hands through the sand. Chloe picks up a bowl and begins to fill it up using a large scoop.

Natasha picks up a sieve and fills it with sand. She watches as the sand runs through leaving the seed in the sieve. She picks up a scoop and attempts to use it to move the seed from the sieve to a yogurt pot. Her concentration shows on her face but very little seed goes into the scoop. She leans over to the tray of utensils and selects a spoon which she uses to carefully transfer the seed. After six spoonfuls she tips the rest of the seed into the pot allowing it to spill over the sides back into the tray. She puts down the sieve, picks up the scoop and moves round to the other side of the table.

Chloe: 'This is my side.'

She looks round but there are no adults looking. She picks up the sieve.

Natasha takes it from her saying: 'That's mine' and walks back to her own side.

Chloe fills a dish and turns to the teacher saying: 'Look at this.'

Ryan walks up to the tray and starts to dig.

Natasha: 'Teacher . . . there's three, there's only supposed to be two.'

Ryan walks away.

Natasha: 'Shall we get all the toys out and collect all the seeds?'

She starts to collect all the utensils and put them on the tray, watched by Chloe. She starts to sieve the sand and tip the seeds into a corner of the tray.

'We'll just have seeds, shall we?'

Chloe picks up a sieve and begins to do the same.

Natasha: 'I'm going to nanny's house for lunch - no dinner.'

Chloe: 'I've got some more seeds for you.'

They pick up individual seeds using a pincer grasp for about two minutes.

Natasha puts some seeds in a pot and brings them over to me: 'Here is a cake for you.'

We talk about the cake.

A child who is deaf comes up to me and attracts my attention by rubbing my cheek. He indicates that he wants to play in the sand.

Chloe looks across and says: 'NO, Natasha is still here.'

Natasha returns to the sand then brings back another pot of seed with a lid on.

Chloe walks over to me and says: 'You know what? I've got a C.H.L.O.E. in my name.'

Natasha offers me the pot of seeds: 'I've made a big cake . . . no I'll open it as it's full up.'

The children walk back to the sand but teacher announces that it is clear-up time.

When you have completed your list of comments about the children, compare it with the suggestions given at the end of the chapter (p. 37). Try not to look too soon. You will notice that the list has been arranged into different areas of development. If you try to think in these terms you will probably find it easier to identify areas you wish to observe.

So now you have several reasons for observing these children. However, if you focus on *one* area of development you can look and record in more detail. Go back and look at the observation again. You

Figure 2.2 That's a picture of me

Figure 2.3

Figure 2.4

Figure 2.5

Figure 2.6

can see that although there is a lot happening, there are also a lot of gaps. Unless you were looking for social interaction it would probably be better to concentrate on one child and look at one area of development – e.g. language, intellectual/cognitive skills, fine manipulative skills, imaginative play. (See Chapter 7 for more details of developmental areas.)

Activity

Figures 2.2 to 2.6 show children and young people aged from 3 to 13 years in various activities. In each situation, choose to observe either a single child or the whole group, then suggest what you might want to find out. Try to formulate specific Aims and Objectives, but if you find this difficult discuss your ideas with your tutor before you decide how to proceed.

Handy tip If you are stuck for ideas try looking at the section on developmental milestones in Chapter 7, or any child development book, and see what children are expected to do at the various ages. This should help you formulate your ideas for Aims and Objectives.

Remember, *Aims* and *Objectives* are just the formal way of setting out your plan to discover what children are able to do. For example, your *Aim* could be to observe a teacher talking to a child. Your *Objectives* could be to discover if the child listened to what was being said and if they could understand what was being asked. This would be written as:

Aim	To observe the class teacher communicating with a 4-year-old.
Objectives	1. To identify the child's ability to listen to a simple request.
	2. To identify the child's ability to carry out a simple request.

Your aim could be to see how children organize an activity. This could be written as:

Aim	To observe a group of Year 6 children (aged 11) planning a drama exercise.
Objectives	1. To identify how well the children are able to work together.
	2. To see if all the children become involved.
	3. To see if any of the children become the leader.

Or your aim could be to see how good children's physical abilities are:

Aim	To observe the gross motor skills of a group of 8–12-year-olds engaged in physical play in the adventure playground.
Objectives	To identify how well they are able to: balance; move between objects; control their movements when using the equipment.
	You might also observe if they worked together to achieve an object.
	This observation could be useful when discussing with the group how they would like the area to be set up.

Activity

Now that you have successfully formulated a variety of Aims and Objectives for the children in the photographs, it is time to try out some of the techniques in your own environment. You could try out one of the examples you used in the last activity, or construct some more of your own for the age group that you work with. You will have noticed that the Aim often refers to the age of the child so it will be important to record the exact age in years and months. This is especially important in the younger age groups where there is a lot of change taking place in a year. Your Objectives for a child who is just 3 years old are unlikely to be the same as for a child who is 3 years and 11 months, as their development should be closer to that of a 4-year-old.

In the first instance it might be a good idea to think of an observation in each of the areas of development. So for the age group that you have chosen write out an Aim and Objectives for:

- fine and gross motor skills
- intellectual/cognitive development
- language skills
- social skills
- emotional development.

If you are working with children over the age of 8 the most likely areas to interest you would be behaviour and how they are using equipment, as they are regularly tested for intellectual development and language through the Key Stage system. (Refer to Chapter 7 if you need help in identifying the areas of development.)

When you have planned your observations, discuss them with your supervisor to make sure they will be possible in the framework of the nursery or classroom routine. There are many pre-set goals to be met, especially those laid down by the National Curriculum, so it may not always be convenient for you to introduce some of your ideas. However, a compromise is usually possible.

Having established what you are going to do, set aside a convenient time and begin to record your observations.

You will now have a collection of observations which focus on an area of development. The next step is to look at what use you can make of them.

The first thing you need to consider is whether the Objectives have been met. This is discussed in the *Conclusion* by looking again at what you have observed and matching it to what you hoped to find out.

There follows an example of an observation with a Conclusion. The format also includes details of the child, such as name and age, and details of the setting. We have also noted the time the observation started and finished.

Observation

Name of child Susan   **Age** 9 months

                              Time commenced 5.15 p.m.

Time completed 5.25 p.m.

Setting The bathroom of the family home.

Aim To observe a 9-month-old baby during bathing.

Objectives To identify and record the child's physical skills.

To identify and record the child's interaction with the adult carer.

Record of observation

The nanny lays Susan on a towel on the floor and starts to undress her. Susan concentrates on the adult face and appears to be listening to her as she explains what she is doing.

'Let's take this jumper off, shall we?'

The nanny pulls the jumper over Susan's head and says 'Boo!'. Susan squeals with delight. She lies quite still as the nanny unfastens the dungarees and pulls them off, then removes the vest.

Susan starts to wriggle and attempts to roll over. The nanny gives her a rattle which gains her attention and she lies quite still, holding it in front of her while the nappy is removed.

As she is lifted into the bath she drops the rattle onto the floor.

Once in the bath Susan picks up the sponge and puts it in her mouth. She begins to suck it and splutters in surprise as the water goes down her throat. She turns and moves onto her knees and grasps the handle on the side of the bath. She pulls herself up into the standing position and leans over the edge. The nanny sits her down in the water again and gives her a plastic book to look at. Susan passes the book from one hand to the other and then puts it in her mouth. She drops it into the water and looks around for something else. The nanny fills a plastic bottle by pushing it under the water. Susan watches the bubbles and laughs, then begins to shout 'da-da-da'.

'Is Daddy coming home soon?'

Susan begins to grizzle and rub her eyes, so nanny quickly finishes washing her and then puts out her hands. Susan holds up her arms to be lifted out.

Conclusion

Susan was very mobile during the observation. She wanted to roll over when she was on the floor and she pulled herself up in the bath.

She was able to hold an object in her hand and pass it into the other hand.

Susan responded to the language used and joined in the game of Peek-a-boo. She co-operated by lifting her arms when it was time to come out of the bath.

You can see how the Conclusion summarizes what you have observed and relates the findings to the Objectives.

Activity

Look back at the previous activity and write Conclusions for your own observation.

_____

_____

_____

_____

This activity almost completes what you should include in a written/narrative observation. You now need to consider how observations can help your work practice by reinforcing your knowledge of child development, and help the children in your care by identifying experiences which will lead them forward.

The value of observations is in their use, not just for a collection in a file. We make use of the observation by evaluating it, comparing it to the expected developmental stage and then making any recommendations. It is possible to compare the development with the other children of a similar age, but it is more usual to refer to a recognized source.

For example:

Observation

Name of child Frederick   **Age** 6 years 3 months

Time commenced 10.45 a.m.

Time completed 10.53 a.m.

Date   1.3.2006

Setting Infant school hall, a class of 25 Year 1 children, a teacher and a classroom assistant. The hall is large and has gym equipment attached to the wall on one side. There is a tape player playing classical music. The lesson is to last 40 minutes. F will be observed for 10 minutes.

Aim   To observe a child's physical development during a National Curriculum dance lesson using a 'descriptive technique'.

Objective To identify if child F is given opportunities to achieve Key Stage 1 attainment targets for physical education.

Record of observation

J crouches with his hands wrapped around legs and his head facing the floor, waiting for the music to start. It does and J lifts his head up and brings his arms out so he is stretching his fingers horizontally, he slowly tries to stand up, but he almost loses his balance so he steadies himself using his right arm. F slowly stands up by straightening his knees and eventually ends up with a star shape on the ground. The music is stopped. The teacher says, 'Very good everyone, now listen to this bit of the piece and try to follow what it tells you to do.' The teacher plays the next extract and this time the music is loud with a strong beat, it is getting louder and louder and faster and faster. F stands still and closes his eyes to listen to the music. When the teacher plays the music again and the children have to move, F jumps up and down three times and then runs a bit like a gorilla, by hanging his hands down low and taking giant steps. He skips about three steps then runs, flapping his arms. The music suddenly goes very quiet and a high-pitched melody can be heard. F stands and listens. The music grows louder again - F crouches down and then starts hopping around the room. He moves his arms as if he is flying very fast, using wings.

Conclusion

I found that F is able to run confidently. He can also hop, skip and jump. He can move imaginatively responding to music, changing direction and expressing feelings in his movement at different speeds and levels.

Evaluation

Tassoni et al. (2002, p. 169) state that: 'Age 6 to 7 "Runs"'. From the observation it is clear that F is able to run, showing that F is reaching this developmental norm. Also: 'Age 6 to 7 "Hops, skips and jumps confidently."' F is also able to complete these developmental norms.

The National Curriculum, Key Stage 1 (5-7 years) (DfEE, 1999, p. 131) states that during dance activities pupils should be taught to:

- Use movement imaginatively, responding to stimuli including music, and performing basic skills (for example - travelling, being still, making a shape, jumping, turning and gesturing).

- Change the rhythm, speed, and level and direction of their movements.

- Create and perform dances using simple movement patterns, including those from other cultures and times.

- Express and communicate ideas and feelings.

During the observation F is given the opportunity to move imaginatively, respond to stimuli, being still, making a shape, jumping, turning and gesturing. F is capable of moving imaginatively, especially moving on different levels at different speeds. F made good shapes and is capable of expressing and communicating ideas and feelings about the music he heard. This shows that F is successfully reaching the developmental norms for dance activities. The attainment targets for children in Key Stage 1 range from level 1 to 3. On average, children should have reached level 2 at the end of this stage. F used a variety of skills, actions and ideas to create his movement piece and is clearly within normal limits.

The method used for the observation was descriptive. The advantages of using this method is that it is relatively easy and can be undertaken on the spur of the moment. The disadvantages are that descriptive observations tend to be shorter and a full picture is not always obtained. Another method that could have been used is a checklist, which is easy for recording purposes but requires forward planning. A checklist provides the observer with closed data that cannot easily be interpreted at a later date - so it is advisable to add comments to clarify. In this instance the descriptive method was effective and met the objectives of this observation.

Recommendations

Maslow's hierarchy of needs (1970) states that children need to have their lower level needs met, before they can achieve the higher level needs such as self-esteem, cognitive needs and self-actualization. Providing F with physical play and activity gives him the opportunity to work towards his higher level needs being met by his achieving success at the lower levels. By helping part of F's physiological needs the school can help develop the rest of his needs.

According to Skinner in Beith et al. (2005), it is a good idea to use positive reinforcement to promote children's learning. If an adult praises F on an individual basis for his efforts in the dance lesson, then his self-esteem will grow. F took the lesson seriously and achieved a good display that he could have demonstrated to the rest of the class. This would also have given him the opportunity to succeed to the level 3 attainment target. This would set F in readiness for his next step, Key Stage 2 in junior school. Asking the children to talk about their dances, to show their dances in small groups or individually and to ask children who were watching to give feedback would promote all the children's learning.

Activity

You can now complete your own observations by making the final evaluation. Look at your *Aims* and *Objectives*, read through your observations and make sure you have summarized them in the *Conclusion*. Look at the *Stage/Level of normal development* for the age group and make a *Comparison* with your findings. The previous example refers to stages described in books you will find listed in the bibliographies, but you can use the milestones given in Chapter 7.

Points to remember

- Be specific in your comments.
- Do not make sweeping statements or assumptions about a child.
- Try always to be objective in your findings.

Finally, you should make any recommendations for further observation or activities. In order to give you some ideas for progression in developmental areas we have included a few examples in Chapter 6. No doubt you will be able to think of many more.

The exercises you have accomplished should have enabled you to complete your structured written/narrative observations – that is, observations which have been planned to discover the abilities of a child or children in a certain developmental area: observations which have predetermined Aims and Objectives. Once you have been recording these for a while and discovered their value you may want to use them to note language or behaviour which just happens around you. This would mean writing without specifically formulated Objectives although it is likely that what interested you was related to one area of development. This would be called an *unplanned* or *unstructured* written/narrative observation. In fact, although it was unplanned it should have a structure. The format should still include details of the child so that conclusions, evaluations and recommendations can be made.

For example:

Observation

Date   5.4.2006

Names of children Samuel and Katie

Ages   Samuel 8 years 1 month Katie 2 years 4 months.

Time commenced 10.15 a.m.

Time completed 10.35 a.m.

Setting Playing in a home environment with a doll's house.

Record of observation

Katie is lying on her front looking into the doll's house. 'Daddy in bed,' she says to herself. She looks at Samuel and repeats, 'Daddy in bed'.

Samuel is not listening and continues to read his book.

Katie continues to play. She walks round to the front of the doll's house and looks in through the window. Suddenly she says, 'Sam, look. I can see Sam in the dolls house.' Sam continues to read his book, but he has obviously heard Katie as he smiles and looks over the top of it.

Katie shouts, 'Sam, Sam, come and look.'

Sam moves off his chair and sits a little closer to the doll's house.

Katie stands up and takes a figure out of the doll's house to show Sam.

Sam looks at it and asks, 'Who is this?' 'It's Daddy,' replies Katie.

Sam moves over to the doll's house and begins to play with Katie. He starts to move the figures around and decide what they are doing. He talks to Katie as they both interact in the make-believe play.

Katie is concentrating well with the input from Sam.

Sam's older brother enters the room.

Sam moves quickly back to his seat and picks up his book, leaving Katie to play alone.

Conclusion

Katie was happy acting out her observations of family life but wanted to involve Sam.

Sam ignored her initially - possibly because he considered playing with a doll's house was 'for girls'. Eventually Katie managed to interest him in her game, and he appeared to enjoy himself - actually taking the lead with the toy figures.

When Sam saw his brother come into the room he quickly moved away from the doll's house and resumed his reading.

Evaluation

According to the developmental milestones collated in Chapter 7, the 2-year-old 'engages in simple role- or make-believe play'. Katie appears to be operating well within the range of expected behaviour.

According to Beith et al. (2005) children at 7-9 years show 'clear differences in play activities that interest boys and girls, for example boys might enjoy kicking a ball around while girls prefer acting out characters'. Sam may have felt that his brother would think playing with a doll's house was for girls. Children will often look up to others and seek their approval at this time.

Recommendations

It would be a good idea to explain to Sam that it is all right to help younger children with their play. He could be made to feel important, especially if praised in front of his brother.

Figure 2.7 Sharing the dolls' house

You have therefore made use of your observation even though you had no set objectives at the outset. It cannot be stressed too often that observations are tools to be used to assist your learning and provide a basis for planning children's progression.

You should now be ready to move on to other forms of recording. These will be discussed in the next chapter.

Suggestions for answers to the second 'Activity' (page 24)

Some of the things you might have learned about Chloe by reading the observation are:

Physical
Good fine manipulative skills – pincer grasp.
Good eye–hand co-ordination using implements.

Intellectual
Good concentration.
Understands concept of number.
Understands mimed gestures.
Shows imaginative skills – seeds in the pot become a cake.
Can spell out the letters of own name.
Language essentially correct in pronunciation and tense.

Social
Works well with others to collect seed.

Emotional
Quite stable and independent.
Not very willing to share.
Still likes the attention of an adult.

REFERENCES

DfEE (1999) *The National Curriculum*. London: DfEE.

Maslow, A.H. (1970) *Motivation and Personality* (2nd edn). New York: Harper & Row.

Skinner, D. (2005) 'Support children's development' in Beith, K., Tassoni, P., Bulmer, K. and Robinson, M. (eds) *Children's Care, Learning and Development*. Oxford: Heinemann.

Tassoni, P., Beith, K., Eldridge, H. and Gough, A. (2002) *Diploma: Child Care and Education*. Oxford: Heinemann.

Vygotsky, L.S. (1978) *Mind and Society: The Development of Higher Mental Processes*. Cambridge MA: Harvard University Press.

CHAPTER THREE

Experimenting with Observational Techniques

At the end of this chapter you will be able to:

- Record your observations in a variety of ways.

- Recognize the strengths and weaknesses of each method.

Now that you have practised the art of observing and interpreting the content from observations in written/narrative form, it is time to look at the variety of other methods in more detail. As a childcare practitioner you are fortunate to have the opportunity to use a wide range of methods, and to gain a realistic awareness of their strengths and weaknesses.

Figure 3.1 shows four methods that can be used: diagrammatic, sampling, written and checklists. From this you should be able to see the learning you can achieve by observing children and young people in a structured way. However, whichever method you use to carry out your observation, it will require the same preliminary information (name, age, date, time), and an evaluation and conclusion as described in the written/narrative form. There is always a reason for undertaking the observation. Once it is completed you would normally make an evaluation and recommendations based around what you have read and reflections on your own work practice. Remember that your evaluation should be based on your knowledge of children's development and should never be judgemental. If you are in doubt about what children and young people should be doing at a certain age, then refer to the milestones given in Chapter 7. However, remember that children of the same age may have had different experiences and be at different levels. Your recommendations should be for the benefit of the child or young person – you are looking at what they *can do*, and then building on that. If you are observing behaviour then you should be looking for recommendations that will assist the child to have a more positive experience.

If you feel that you have not achieved what you set out to discover by your observation, then you may need to try one of the other methods.

Figure 3.1

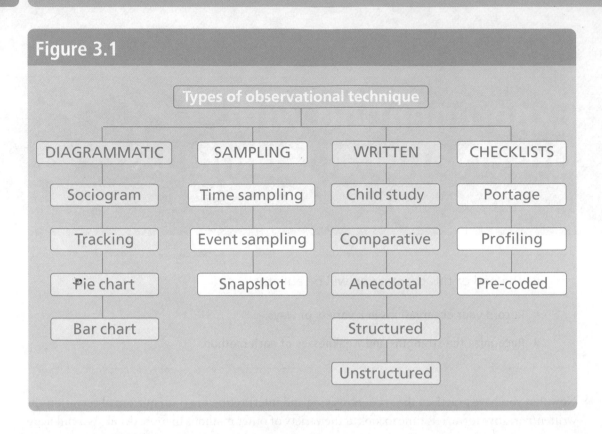

Figure 3.1 sets out some of the formats for recording observation that are commonly used. You will see that the examples build on the information given in Chapter 1.

There follow some suggestions for when you might use the different types of recording techniques.

Diagrammatic

Sociogram: Observing and recording children's social behaviour by plotting their interactions or compiling a graph of their expressed friendships.

Tracking: Observing and recording a child's or children's movements around a limited area for a length of time, e.g. classroom, nursery, adventure playground.

Pie chart: An alternative method of recording a time sampling observation or bar chart.

Bar/Block chart: A pictorial method of recording an observation of a whole group's ability to undertake a specific task, or a way of showing blocks of time spent on an activity.

Sampling

Time sampling: Observing and recording what a child or young person is doing every minute for a short time, e.g. 10 minutes, or at intervals during a set period of time, e.g. every 15 minutes over a morning or afternoon.

Event sampling: Observing and recording certain events as they occur, e.g. aggressive behaviour or temper tantrums.

Snapshot: Observing and recording events at a particular moment. They are useful for comparing use of equipment at different times of the day or monitoring play areas in order to make the best use of equipment.

Written

Child study: Observing a child over a period of time to evaluate their overall developmental progress. This will normally include some details of the child's background and always needs parental permission.

Comparative: There are two main types of comparative observation: observing two children or young people and comparing their abilities, or observing a child over a period of time in order to evaluate their progress.

Anecdotal/Diary: A record of a child over a period of time that consists of a series of unstructured observations.

Structured: Observing and recording for a specific purpose with pre-planned aim and objectives, e.g. capabilities of a child entering school, or ability to do a specific task, e.g. carry out a science experiment.

Unstructured: Observing children or young people without a predetermined aim. This type of observation is spontaneous and usually comes about as a result of something interesting or unexpected occurring. It may be more difficult to evaluate but could provide you with recommendations for a further observation or encourage you to reflect upon your own work practice. It is a reason for keeping a notebook and pencil in your pocket.

Checklists

Observing and recording specific aspects of development using a pre-coded checklist of developmental milestones. This may be an individual observation, but often forms part of an overall and ongoing profile of the child. The profiling record of children during the foundation stage consists of checklists that are supported by short written observations. This allows the practitioner to comment on 'how' and 'when' a child does something.

Checklists are also commonly used when working with special needs children in order to monitor their progress. Portage is a system that breaks down the milestones into smaller steps which are used to develop a plan for the practitioners and parents to work with the child. Checklists are then used to monitor how successfully the targets are being met. This enables the practitioners and parents to set new targets or redefine the task.

SATs are checklists of attainment set by the government in England and Wales to monitor children's progress. At present children are tested at 7, 11 and 14 in England, but were abolished at 11 and 14 for children in Wales in 2004. These tests are set so that children can be assessed to see what level they are working at. They do only measure ability to complete questions. If children fail to reach the minimum standard, then more observations need to be carried out to try to determine what the problem is, and what support could be given. For example, has the child got a problem with 'reading the question', 'understanding what they have read' or 'formulating and writing the answer'?

For more information about SATs you can visit www.qca.org.uk

Readers in Scotland can look at www.sqa.org.uk and those in the Republic of Ireland can go to www.nqai.ie/en/

Other countries and organizations have similar systems on which to base their educational or social targets.

You might also consider using different media to help you record your observation, but this should always be discussed with your supervisor in the interest of confidentiality, as film or tape will obviously make the child and setting more obvious.

Figure 3.2 below shows you some of the different recording media you might use.

It is not possible to demonstrate the use of video or tape in this book, but the following examples are written in different formats for you to use as reference. At the end of the chapter there are some suggested Aims and Objectives for you to decide which method would be most suitable to enable you to assess the abilities of the child or children you are observing.

Figure 3.2 Different media for recording observations

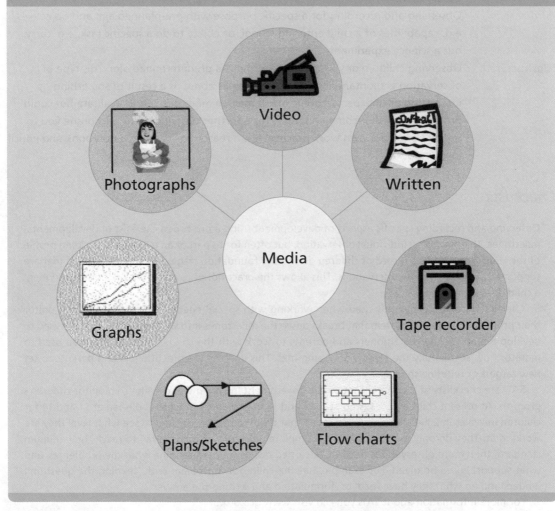

Diagrammatic

Tracking

As stated in Chapter 1, the usual reason for undertaking a tracking observation is to record the time a child spends with an activity or the number of activities they choose. The following example illustrates its use to track a child to discover motor skills on a choice of apparatus. Before commencing, you will need to draw a plan of the area that you are going to observe the child in. You will need to consider how you are going to record the movement, e.g. do you need to devise a code? You will also need to think about your Objectives and how they can be met. In the example in Chapter 1 (p. 7), the Objectives were likely to have been connected to the time the child spent on the activity, so it was important to note times on the diagram. In the following example you will see that the principal objective is to discover which apparatus is chosen. You do not, therefore, need to note time. However, there is a second Objective: to identify the skills used on the apparatus. There is not usually space on the diagram to write this, especially if you identify any difficulties. You will therefore need to note this down separately.

Observation

Date of observation 22.3.2006   **Time commenced** 10.50 a.m.

                                     Time completed 11.05 a.m.

Number of children Whole class

Number of adults 2

Name of child Adrian   **Age** 6 years exactly

Aim   To observe a 6-year-old while in a formally arranged setting of the gymnastic apparatus in the school hall.

Objectives To track the choice of apparatus used.

       To identify and record Adrian's gross motor skills while using apparatus.

Setting The school hall set out for a PE lesson to be used by the whole class.

Record of observation

Ropes Some difficulty climbing onto the end of the rope and not able to swing successfully, but spends several minutes trying.

Hoops, balances, horse Not used.

Climbing frame Most time spent here. Climbs quite well initially but rather hesitant near the top of the frame. Descending is rather a problem. Adrian feels carefully for each rung before moving.

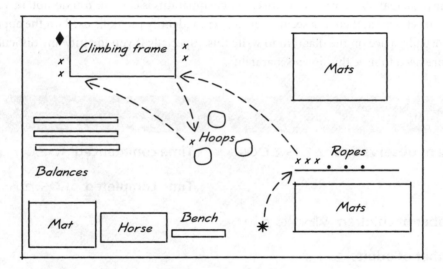

Figure 3.3 Tracking observation

Conclusion

From the tracking observation it is obvious that Adrian prefers to work on the large apparatus – either the climbing frame or the ropes, and avoiding the balances and horse. Adrian found difficulty in climbing onto the knot of the rope and then swinging. On the climbing frame he moved alternate arms and legs, reaching up above his head with arms extended and carefully watching where he was going. However, he appeared hesitant and apprehensive when near the top of the frame. The higher he climbed, the less fluent were his movements and he stopped several times to watch other children. He climbed down apprehensively, feeling for each rung before making a move.

Evaluation

According to Catherine Lee (1990, p. 186), a typical 6-year-old 'enjoys using large apparatus for climbing, swinging by arms, hanging by knees. Can somersault, skip with a rope, run and jump and use climbing ropes.' Although Adrian is keen to participate in these activities and likes to use the large apparatus, he has not yet gained confidence, and is unable to move fluently as most children of this age would be able to do. Most children enjoyed the vigorous physical play and used their bodies confidently and actively. Adrian appeared hesitant and apprehensive and enjoyed activities that he had some success with and returned to these, unlike most 6-year-olds, who are keen to master new skills and practise until they perfect them.

Recommendations

Adrian needs more activities to gain self-confidence. He also needs more practice in physical activities and should be encouraged to participate in all the apparatus work and free-standing activities.

This record shows very clearly the value of observing children as individuals. In the general rush of the class activity it is easy to miss the fact that one child is having some difficulty. Experienced workers will usually spot that a child needs some extra help, but it is always useful to have recorded proof.

Sociogram

The sociogram records the social contacts a single child makes, or the friendships among a group of children. It is interesting to undertake, but is subject to considerable distortion. A normally outgoing child may have a day when they are happy to be by themselves. Children often make and break friendships. These things should be remembered when drawing up conclusions. However, sociograms are interesting to test out the theories that young children are more likely to have changing friends, while teenagers have a special companion whom they are able to share all their concerns with.

There are several ways that a sociogram can be recorded. For the individual child, time sampling (p. 40) or tracking are probably the best. This will show how many contacts a child makes during a set period of time. In the classroom situation, children usually work in groups of similar ability and are not encouraged to move about, so it is best to observe social contacts during playtime.

In order to complete a sociogram on a group of children you can ask them to draw, write or tell you about their friendships. This may depend on their ages.

Observation

Group sociogram of friendships

Date   8.3.2006

Number of children 15   **Ages** 10 years 10 months to 11 years 7 months

Setting A primary school, Year 6, in the classroom.

Aim   To discover the friendship groups in the class.

Objectives To discover if boys and girls mix in their friendships.

To record if some children are more popular.

Record of observation
Each child was given a piece of paper and asked to write down who their 'two best friends' were. Several children asked if they could have three, but were limited to only two. Figure 3.4 shows the results; all the children in the class are included. The names on the vertical axis were chosen by those in the boxes.

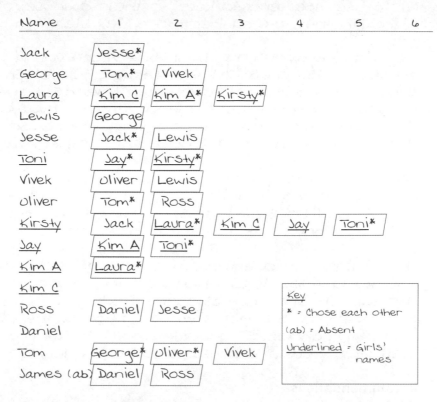

Name	1	2	3	4	5	6
Jack	Jesse*					
George	Tom*	Vivek				
Laura	Kim C	Kim A*	Kirsty*			
Lewis	George					
Jesse	Jack*	Lewis				
Toni	Jay*	Kirsty*				
Vivek	Oliver	Lewis				
Oliver	Tom*	Ross				
Kirsty	Jack	Laura*	Kim C	Jay	Toni*	
Jay	Kim A	Toni*				
Kim A	Laura*					
Kim C						
Ross	Daniel	Jesse				
Daniel						
Tom	George*	Oliver*	Vivek			
James (ab)	Daniel	Ross				

Key
* = Chose each other
(ab) = Absent
Underlined = Girls' names

Figure 3.4 Record of observation

Conclusion

All the girls chose same-sex friends, as did most of the boys. The only exception was Jack, who chose Kirsty. Several of the children chose each other – this is shown by an asterisk by the name in the box*. Kirsty was chosen most often. Two children were not chosen by any of the other children, and one child who was absent was chosen twice.

Evaluation

The group tended to choose children of the same sex. This has been noted by Valda Reynolds (1994) when discussing younger children: 'By the age of 7 or 8 the child will be very much aware of sexual differences. Boys of this age usually prefer to be involved in traditional masculine games and activities, keeping mainly in the company of boys.

Girls likewise tend to keep to their own sex, although they are rather more flexible than boys.'

Donald Greydanus (1997) writing about young adolescents notes: 'At this stage of development they may or may not have many friends, but they'll probably want one best friend, almost always of the same sex.' This may be one of the reasons that many of the group chose each other.

It is interesting that some of the teasing in class is about having 'a girlfriend', but there is little evidence of boys and girls chatting to each other, although they work together on projects.

The children chosen the most are all outgoing and usually take the lead when working in groups. Of the two children not chosen, the boy is not a surprise – he is bigger than the rest of the class and often chooses to work alone. The girl works well in a group and appears to have friends.

Recommendations
Although the results were much as expected, it would be interesting to repeat the observation at the end of the academic year, when the children will be moving to different secondary schools.

Bar chart

In Chapter 1 we looked at the bar chart as a method of recording a class's ability to complete a task. In the following example, the bar chart is used to give a pictorial representation of the time spent on different activities during a typical day's routine for twins. The times are recorded throughout the day and then transferred to the chart.

Observation

Date of observation 14.9.2006   **Time commenced** 9.00 a.m.
                                     Time completed 4.30 p.m.

Number of adults 2

Number of children 2

Names of children Aidan   **Age** 1 year 2 months
                      Marc   1 year 2 months

Setting Throughout the house.

Aim To observe the care plan of 1-year-old twins throughout the day.

Objective To record in minutes the amount of time spent on social care and play on a typical day.

Record of observation

Time	Activity
9.00 - 9.10 a.m.	Play in the playroom.
9.10 - 9.15 a.m.	Nappy change.
9.15 - 9.30 a.m.	Play in the playroom.
9.30 - 9.40 a.m.	Snack time.
9.40 - 10.15 a.m.	Play in the playroom.
10.15 - 10.30 a.m.	Face washing and dressing for outdoors.
10.30 - 12 noon	Outing to the park.
12 noon - 12.15 p.m.	Watch TV.
12.15 - 12.45 p.m.	Lunch.
12.45 - 1.10 p.m.	Garden play.
1.10 - 1.20 p.m.	Wash and nappy change.
1.20 - 3.05 p.m.	Sleep and rest.
3.05 - 3.10 p.m.	Nappy change.
3.10 - 3.20 p.m.	Play in the playroom.
3.20 - 3.30 p.m.	Snack time.
3.30 - 4.30 p.m.	Play in the playroom.

Conclusion

The majority of the twins' day consisted of playtime and outings - 250 minutes. Children of this age still require a daytime sleep - 105 minutes. Apart from a short period watching TV, the rest of the day was taken up by washing and feeding - 85 minutes.

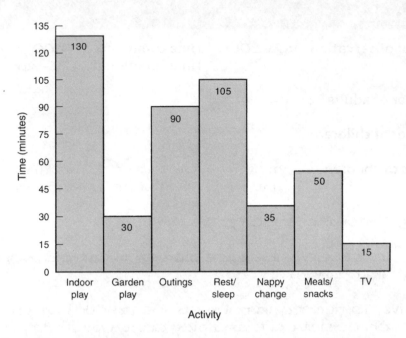

Figure 3.5 Bar graph showing time spent on each activity throughout the day

Evaluation

The day care programme followed by this family is very similar to one recommended by Patricia Geraghty (1988), who states in the section about planning a child's day: 'The core of the programme for the young child in day care is play, balanced by regular times allotted for routines such as washing, lunch, snacks and a rest period.'

Recommendations

In order to evaluate the quality of the children's daily routine some detailed written/narrative observations of the play should be carried out.

Pie chart

Pie charts are a pictorial way of showing a period of time or a number of children divided up into percentages of a circle (360 degrees). It would be possible to show the bar graph in the previous example in a pie chart format.

In Chapter 1 we looked at pie charts as a way of illustrating percentages of the class who could carry out a procedure. In this example we are using the chart to show the amount of time a child spends on different activities. This can cover any length of time, but it is likely that the younger the child, the shorter the time, as younger children are more liable to have a shorter attention span for one activity.

Observation

Date of observation 7.4.2006   **Time commenced** 10.45 a.m.
                                     Time completed 11.00 a.m.

Number of adults 1   **Number of children** 3

Name of child Joseph   **Date of birth** 21.10.2002
                                     Age 3 years, 6 months

Aim   To observe a 3½-year-old during a free-choice
            session.

Objectives To observe and record his concentration span
            at different activities.

Setting In the quiet area of the nursery, which had been
            set out with various activities.

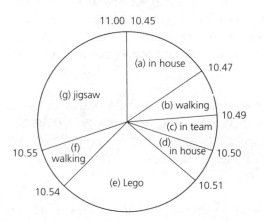

Figure 3.6 Pie chart showing percentage of time on each activity.   Joseph in the house

Record of observation

(a) Joseph goes into the home corner and begins to make dinner. He gets a dish out of the cupboard and searches through the food basket to find the pizza. He puts the pizza into the dish and then puts it into the oven. 'It's hot now,' he says. He goes over to the drawer and gets out the oven glove. He uses this to lift the pizza out of the oven and put it on the table. He takes off the oven glove and puts it next to the pizza, then he walks away.

(b-c) Joseph walks aimlessly around the room and finally stops at the Lego. He puts both hands into the Lego box and moves the bricks around, while watching Daniel, who has moved to the doll's house. Joseph moves over towards the train set and crouches down, watching Matthew pushing a train along. He stands up and steps over the railway track, then turns towards the doll's house.

(d) Joseph kneels and picks up the ladder with his right hand. He bends over and carefully places the ladder midway between the first and ground floor of the house. He moves around the doll's house on his knees, and when almost completely around the house he stands up and moves back to the Lego table.

(e) Joseph stands by the side of the Lego table and picks up a small piece using the thumb and finger of his right hand. He puts it onto the table and pushes it down using the same two fingers. He repeats this three more times before moving away from the table.

(f) Joseph walks round the room without taking much notice of what is laid out on the various tables. The nursery nurse suggests that he might like to do a jigsaw puzzle and he answers: 'Yes' and walks over to the table.

(g) Joseph sits down at the jigsaw table with the nursery nurse. He removes the pieces from the puzzle board, using his thumb and index finger. He begins to put the pieces back into the correct spaces. He does not need help but looks to the nursery nurse for encouragement at intervals. He completes the puzzle and smiles.

Conclusion

When given a free choice of activities Joseph took some time in choosing, and even when he settled to an activity it could not hold his attention span for longer than a few minutes, after which he would get up and walk around the room before stopping briefly to play with another activity. With the help of an adult Joseph found it easier to settle and concentrate.

Evaluation

Joseph has been attending nursery for only half a term and is still overwhelmed by the wide choice of activities available. After he was offered guidance and felt reassured, he sat and concentrated well. Having been in nursery for such a short time he is just beginning to explore the nursery environment, and prefers to stand and watch other children rather than join in himself. He says very little and appears not to have reached the stage where he 'joins in play with other children in and outdoors', described by Mary Sheridan (1975).

Recommendations

Joseph will need to be provided with activities which will extend his concentration. For the time being he needs to be guided and limited in his choice. He also needs to be encouraged to join in small group activities.

Pie chart in a differing format

In the previous observation the pie chart showed the time spent on each activity as a percentage of the total time in the diagram, and then the written element described what took place during each segment of time.

It is also possible to record the activities directly onto the chart. This is obviously easier if there are fewer segments.

The following example is for an observation of similar length to the first, but on a child who stayed longer with individual activities.

Observation

Date of observation 20.7.2006 **Time commenced** 10.40 a.m.

Time completed 10.57 a.m.

Number of adults 1 **Number of children** 1

Name of child Rupert **Date of birth** 16.6.2002
Age 4 years 1 month

Aim To observe a 4-year-old's choice of activity during free play.

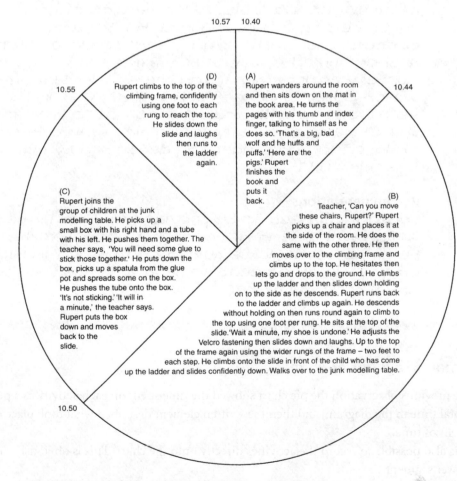

Figure 3.7 Record of information in different pie chart format

Objectives To observe and record the concentration span and physical development of a 4-year-old.

Setting In a nursery which has various activities arranged for the children to choose. In one corner there is a climbing frame, which includes a slide. There is a junk modelling table being directed by the teacher, and painting and number games are also available.

Conclusion

Rupert chose to be busy during his 'free-choice' period. He began with a quiet activity – looking at a book, and delighted in the pictures for a few minutes. He then became interested in the more physical activity of being on the slide. In the beginning he was cautious in his approach to the climbing frame and slide but as he repeated the activity he gained in confidence and enjoyment. He was then interested in junk modelling, but quickly returned to the slide as the modelling did not really go to plan for him.

Evaluation

Rupert showed confidence, purpose and persistence in his ability on the climbing frame and slide. He repeated the activity several times, gained in confidence and concentrated on what he was doing. A typical 4-year-old is 'very agile . . . climbs trees and ladders. Climbs stairs and descends confidently one foot to a stair' (see Chapter 7). Four-year-olds enjoy the opportunity for vigorous play in a safe environment and Rupert demonstrated this. He did not concentrate so long on the quieter activities.

Recommendations

Rupert did not concentrate on the junk modelling task because it proved rather difficult. Opportunities to succeed at fine manipulative skills should be introduced and then further observation made. The concentration span of all children can also be increased by an adult taking an interest in what is happening.

Sampling

Time sampling – target child/ren

Using a target child or children for an observation concentrates on making a detailed record of the behaviour and language of one or two children. Advantages of using the time sampling method on one or two children rather than the written/descriptive type of observation are that it helps you to focus on:

- Who talked to whom?
- Are the target children following instructions accurately?
- Who initiates social interaction?
- How long did the target child/ren spend on the activity – were they concentrating on the given task?

As stated in Chapter 1, the interval chosen between recordings will depend upon what your Aims and Objectives are.

Observation

Time sampling – Observing two target children

Date of observation 10.3.2006

Time commenced 1.30 p.m.
Time completed 2.05 p.m.

Number of adults 2

Number of children 22

Names of children Alan
Brenda

Age 5 years 10 months
6 years 1 month

Aims To observe two target children, Alan and Brenda, undertaking a curriculum art activity.
To use a time sample observation, observing A and B every 5 minutes for 35 minutes.

Objectives To observe A's and B's attainment levels in National Curriculum Key Stage 1 art and design.

Settings An infant school classroom. The classroom is large and bright. All tables have been covered with newspaper and have five sheets of A2 paper on each table. In the middle are two dishes with blue paint in them and another dish with bits of different objects to print with, e.g. cotton reels, bricks, 2D shapes, corks and combs.

Record of observation

Time (mins)	Place	Activity	Others present	Additional information for A	Additional information for B
5	Classroom on carpet	Teacher talking about making patterns: 'brick patterns, window patterns and rotating patterns'. She shows the class photographs of different houses that they took on their walk around the area. She asks, 'What is the shape of the windows and doors?'	20 children, 1 teacher, 1 student	A answers questions about shapes of windows, doors. A says, 'They look like rectangles.'	Eating carrot looking at the wall.
10	Walking to table	Putting on aprons, finding a chair	20 children, 1 teacher, 1 student	Walks straight to aprons and puts one over his head and asks student, 'Can you do it up for me?'	Stands up and asks the teacher, 'What do I do with the carrot?' Teacher says, 'Put it in the tray or in the bin.'
15	Sitting at table	Printing	5 children, 1 student	A says to B, 'Please can you pass me the triangle? I like that pattern, B, that is really effective.' A prints with triangle edges - triangle on paper.	'Yes.' B blushes and looks down to the floor embarrassed.
20	Standing at table	Printing/washing hands	5 children, 1 student, 1 teacher	A says to teacher, 'I don't like my work, because it is all one colour; I want to use red too.' Teacher says, 'I want you to think about the shapes you are making, not the colour.'	Teacher says, 'B, do not use your hands, go and wash them.' B looks embarrassed and goes to wash her hands.
25	Standing at table	Printing	5 children, 1 student	Using whole shape to print with, then two together.	B printing.
30	Standing at table	Printing	5 children, 1 student	A is using the rotation method of printing.	Student asks, 'Have you thought about what part of the building you are drawing?' B says, 'It's the window.'
35	Standing at table	Printing	5 children, 1 student	A looking at his work.	'I don't like my work, I think it looks really bad, it's really messy.'

Conclusion

1. <u>Exploring and developing ideas</u>

   Pupils should be taught to:

   a. Record from first-hand observation, experience and imagination, and explore ideas.

   b. Ask and answer questions about the starting points for their work, and develop their ideas.

2. <u>Investigating and making art, craft and design</u>

   a. Investigate the possibilities of a range of materials and processes.

   b. Try out tools and techniques and apply these to materials and processes, including drawing.

   c. Represent observations, ideas and feelings, and design and make images and artefacts.

3. <u>Evaluating and developing work</u>

   Pupils should be taught to:

   a. Review what they and others have done and say what they think and feel about it.

   b. Identify what they might change in their current work or develop in their future work.

4. <u>Knowledge and understanding</u>

   a. Visual and tactile elements, including colour, pattern and texture, line and tone, shape, form and space.

   b. Materials and processes used in making art, craft and design.

   c. Differences and similarities in the work of artists, craftspeople and designers in different times and cultures.

5. <u>Breadth of study</u>

During Key Stage 1, pupils should be taught knowledge, skills and understanding through:

a. Exploring a range of topics for practical work (e.g. themselves, their experiences, stories, the local environment).

b. Working on their own, collaborating with others, on projects in two and three dimensions and on different scales.

c. Using a range of materials and processes (e.g. painting, collage, print making and textiles).

d. Investigating different kinds of art, craft and design.

From the observation areas 1a, 1b, 2a, some of 2b, 2c, 3a and some of 3b, some of 4a and some of 5c have been covered in this art activity.

The children in the class were given the opportunities to record from first-hand experiences (they had been for a walk in the areas surrounding the school and the teacher showed the children photographs of different houses before the children started printing). The children were provided with tools and had to use their imagination as to how to use the tools to print different patterns. All the children were asked questions. B answered her question and A made statements and talked about his work.

A and B investigated a range of objects in order to print patterns. This is an example of how the children tried out tools and different techniques and applied them to the processes. B said she did not like her work because it was messy and A said he liked his work except that he wanted to use more than one colour. This indicates that A has been successfully taught 3a. A used different objects to create different patterns; he used tone, shape and space to create the finished piece of work. He decided where to put the printing in order to create his whole painting. B also had the opportunity to use pattern, tone, shape and space in her printing activity; she also repeated shapes around her paper.

Both children had the opportunity to use a range of materials (corks, bricks, 2D shapes) in order to create a print-making process.

Evaluation
The method used for this observation was a time sample observation. The advantage of doing a time sample observation is that this method enables the observer to record in detail over a period of time the activities undertaken by one or two children. This method was effective in meeting the aims of the observation, as it is a structured method of observing a planned curriculum art lesson.

Page 33 of the National Curriculum handbook (DfEE, 1999), art and design, states that:

Level 1

'Pupils respond to ideas. They use a variety of materials and processes to communicate their ideas and meanings, design and make images and artefacts; they describe what they think and feel about their own and others' work.'

Level 2

'Pupils explore ideas. They investigate and use a variety of materials and processes to communicate their ideas and meanings, and design and make images and artefacts. They comment on differences in others' work and suggest ways of improving their own.'

Level 3

'Pupils explore ideas and collect visual and other information for their work. They investigate visual and tactile qualities in materials and similarities and differences between their own and others' work, and adapt and improve their own.'

By the end of Year 1 children are expected to have reached, on average, level 2.

From the observation A has reached level 2 in the attainment target of the National Curriculum Key Stage 1 in art and design. A explored the objects he printed with by using all sides of them; he printed patterns of shapes using the objects that were the same shape. For example, he printed a triangle shape on his paper using sides of a triangle shape. A used all types of printing methods, such as rolling the objects, using edges of the object, using the whole object, printing with two objects. He printed rotating patterns, flowing patterns and random patterns. A said that he did not like his work because it was all one colour; he wanted to use red as well as blue. He also told B that he liked her pattern and that it was really effective. This shows that A was commenting on differences in another's work and suggesting ways in which to improve his own.

B is reaching level 1 according to the attainment targets of the National Curriculum Key Stage 1 in art and design. B responded to ideas as suggested by the student. B used a variety of materials during her printing sessions including her hands, which the teacher asked her not to do as she was to use objects for printing.

Recommendations

Recommendations include giving B more opportunities to experiment with making patterns with lots of different shapes including hands. B should be given support on how to relate it to the project brief and this will help promote her self-esteem and be proud of her achievements. She would also benefit from positive reinforcement, communication and encouragement when she is undertaking challenging tasks.

Talking with children involves the adult using precise, accurate language if we are not to increase their confusion. (Curtis and O'Hagan, 2003, p. 189)

If an adult had talked through the task on a one-to-one basis child B would have been less likely to use her hands to print and possibly would have achieved more effective patterns and shapes in her work.

Child A should have the opportunity to do more printing using a range of equipment and colours and be given the opportunity to create a picture of a house using these prints. Both children would benefit from cutting up their print and making it into a 3D house. They would be developing their fine motor skills and could experiment with their own work. The children would also benefit from more opportunities to experiment with mark making in all forms, not only print making but also rubbings, chalk drawing, ink and wax paintings, drawing from still life and exploring different patterns their body can make. Opportunities for child-child learning to take place should be created. Children should be placed in small specific groups in such a way that they can learn from each other. For example, children with high self-esteem sitting with children of low self-esteem can help promote children's development.

There is an increasing body of research to show that children can learn from each other as well as from adults, particularly when the children are of mixed ages. This type of grouping, which is a characteristic of our nurseries, is a legacy from our childhood educators who were well aware of the value of child–child learning. (Curtis and O'Hagan, 2003, p. 155)

Event sampling

Event sampling is usually linked to observations of children who have a tendency to behave in an anti-social way, such as having temper tantrums or bullying. The aim is to record any incident, what preceded it, and what followed it in order to see if there is any pattern. This will hopefully allow a strategy to be devised to help the child modify their behaviour.

Observation

Date of observation 20.1.2007 **Time** Throughout the day

Number of adults 2   **Number of children** Whole class

Name of child Ben   **Age** 5 years 4 months

Setting Reception class

Aim To observe Ben's behaviour throughout a day in the classroom.

Objectives To record any incidents of anti-social behaviour.

To identify what was taking place before the incident.

To record what happened after the incident.

Conclusion
Ben reacted very quickly if someone aggravated him. He tended to take what he wanted without asking. Ben used very little language throughout the day - he was much more likely to use actions. Ben was not always the first to provoke the incident.

Evaluation
Two of the aspects of the social development of a 4-year-old are described in Chapter 7 (p. 162) as: 'Likes the companionship of other children and adults but alternates between co-operation and conflict; however, understands the need to use words rather than blows.'

Ben is 5 and still tends to use blows rather than words when he is thwarted or unable to have his own way. However, the other children do seem to have learned this and can provoke Ben to retaliate.

Recommendations

Encourage Ben to express his feelings in acceptable ways, e.g. clay, water, role play.

Listen to both children's explanations after an incident.

Reward good behaviour.

Record of observation

Date/Time	Incident	Previous happening	Who was there	What happened next	Comment
20.1.2006 11.20	Ben snatched the rubber from James and James snatched it back.	Writing a story of Ben's choice in work task.	Three other children were present at the table and the teacher was at her desk.	Ben called James a name and hit him on the arm. James shouted and the teacher intervened.	Ben needs to ask politely first; if not, then include the teacher. Ben needs to control his anger.
11.35	Repeat of previous incident.	Continuing to write at the table.	James and Ben were alone at the table. Teacher in book corner.	James called the teacher to intervene and Ben was moved to sit by himself.	Ben reminded again to ask before taking.
1.20	Elliot pushed Ben from behind and Ben fell over.	Children were changing for a PE lesson.	All the children were changing together. Teacher was assisting.	Ben jumped up and pulled Elliot's jumper. Elliot shouted and teacher intervened.	Ben not the initial instigator of the incident.
1.50	Ben screamed because he thought someone had taken his tie.	Children were changing back after PE.	All the children were together.	Several children backed away from Ben looking quite scared. Teacher intervened and found tie.	Ben needs to find an acceptable way to express himself.

Snapshot

As the name suggests, a snapshot observation samples what is happening at a given moment in time in a specific area. The most usual reason for this type of observation is to discover which areas of the nursery or classroom are being used. It can also provide a method of seeing which children are playing together. The method of recording is quite flexible. You can actually take a photograph or series of photographs and study them at a later date. You can draw a diagram of the setting as you would for a tracking observation and mark in where the children are at a certain time, or you can write a description. The following example is a written description of a nursery class.

Snapshot observation

Date 6.6.2006   **Time commenced** 10.15 a.m.

Time completed 10.20 a.m.

Number of children All the children in the nursery.

Ages 2 years 6 months to 4 years.

Number of adults 3

Aim To observe and record what children are involved in doing within the different areas of the nursery.

Objective To alter the arrangement of the activities available, or limit the numbers on some activities if necessary.

Setting The nursery classroom.

Record of observation

The nursery teacher is organizing a finger-painting activity. Sarah, Robert, Philip and Shaheeda are working with her.

The nursery nurse is reading a story to three children - James, Ben and Candy.

Sophie and Jasmin are playing in the sand tray.

Sam, Angela, Helen, Nicola and Neil are in the home corner. Sam and Angela are dressed up as nurses and Nicola has a stethoscope round her neck. Helen and Neil are lying down on the beds.

Julia and Reuben are putting the railway track together and running Thomas the tank engine along it.

Stephanie is wandering from the home corner to the finger-painting activity.

Naomi, Pat and Kelly are being supervised in the water play by the student. They are pouring the water onto a wheel and watching it turn.

Conclusion
All of the children were involved with an activity with the exception of Stephanie, who had just left the home corner for the finger painting. No activity was overcrowded, although the home corner was busy and could not have taken any more children.

Recommendations
There is no need to change the activities at the present time, but the sand and water trays could be moved further apart as the children were a little crowded.

Written/Narrative

The structured and unstructured form of the written narrative were described in Chapter 2. We will now consider the other forms listed at the beginning of this chapter.

Comparative

The comparative observation can be used to evaluate two children of the same age at the same time, and a possible method would be a checklist. For example, you might be assessing the children's ability to carry out tasks or perform physical activities and comparing their results with each other as well as the developmental norms. You could also compare a child's ability on two different occasions. This is often used to monitor any change in behaviour or development when working with special needs children.

The following example illustrates its use to compare a child's ability to indicate a need for the toilet. Children with special needs are regularly monitored, so a baseline is often available if a change is noted. This allows a second observation to be undertaken and an objective evaluation to be made. In the example both the original written/narrative record and the comparative observation are shown.

Original observation

Date   18.1.2006   **Time commenced** 10.25 a.m.
                               Time completed 10.31 a.m.

Number of children 1

Number of adults 1

Name of child Hayley   **Age** 4 years 4 months

Setting   In the toilet area. There are three toilets - the one being used for the observation is lower and has a rail to assist the less able children to be independent.

Aim   To observe a new entrant's ability to use the toilet without assistance.

Objectives To observe and record Hayley's ability to convey a need to use the toilet.
To observe and record Hayley's ability to use the toilet herself.

Record of observation
Hayley is wriggling about and holding herself. She touches the nursery nurse's hand and says something to her. The nursery nurse takes her hand and they walk slowly and rather unsteadily to the toilet together. Once in the toilet area Hayley walks to the adapted cubicle and pushes the door open with her left hand. She walks in, and as she approaches the raised floor she reaches out with her right hand and then places it on the wall before stepping up. Once she has both feet on the raised section she removes her hand and then steps forward before turning around. She stands still and waits. The nursery nurse asks if everything is all right. Hayley smiles and lifts her right hand to point behind the door. The nursery nurse lifts the training seat from behind the door and puts it on the toilet. Hayley has remained quite still, so the nursery nurse encourages her to pull her pants down. Hayley manages to pull down her trousers and pants and the nursery nurse praises

her. Hayley lifts up her arms and the nursery nurse lifts her onto the toilet. Hayley smiles and the nursery nurse says she is going to see the child next door but will be back in a minute. While sitting on the toilet Hayley's back is bent and her head is over her knees. When she has finished using the toilet she wriggles off and shuffles to the edge of the raised floor with her pants and trousers around her ankles. At the end of the raised floor, Hayley reaches for the wall with her left hand and steps down. She continues to shuffle forward until she is just outside the toilet door. The nursery nurse returns and asks Hayley if she has finished. Hayley smiles and nods her head. The nursery nurse kneels down and verbally encourages Hayley to pull her pants up. Making no effort to do so, Hayley nods her head and says 'No'. Invited again to try, Hayley moves closer to the wall and unsteadily proceeds to pull up her pants. She tries to pull up the trousers but is unable to do so. The nursery nurse helps, telling her what a good girl she is.

Conclusion

Hayley is aware of when she needs to use the toilet and is able to tell the nursery nurse.

She needs a lot of encouragement, but is able to pull down her trousers and pants.

She is not able to get on the toilet herself, but is able to be left alone for a short period.

Hayley is able to get off the toilet but makes no attempt to dress herself.

If the clothing is loose, e.g. her pants, Hayley is able to pull it up with encouragement, but with tightly fitting clothes like her trousers she needs help.

Evaluation

Hayley is usually able to make her toileting needs known to an adult although she still occasionally has an accident. Due to her physical disability, which affects her motor skills, balance and co-ordination, Hayley often has difficulty removing tight clothing, and needs constant praise and encouragement from an adult. With reference to Catherine Lee (1990), Hayley should be able to use the toilet independently and should have little or no difficulty in removing her clothing. According to Lee's criteria Hayley is performing at the level of a 2½-year-old who 'still has an occasional accident, but is able to ask the adult for the toilet, before she needs to go immediately'.

Hayley attended the nursery on a morning-only basis for the first term. After the Easter holiday she came full time. It was noticed that she was often found wet when toileted at the usual times, and that she no longer asked to use the bathroom. It was decided to carry out an observation over a period of a week to see if Hayley had regressed since attending the nursery on a full-time basis. The observation would consist of a tick chart which the staff would fill in.

Observation

Date   24.4.2006   **Time commenced** } The week
                            Time completed } 24-28 April

Number of children 1

Number of adults 5

Name of child Hayley   **Age** 4 years 7 months

Setting The nursery and toilet area.

Aim   To re-assess Hayley's ability to ask for and use the toilet.

Objectives To record the number of times Hayley asks to use the toilet.

To record the number of times Hayley uses the toilet successfully.

To record the number of times Hayley is found to be wet.

Record of observation

The staff were asked to record on the chart if they took Hayley to the toilet:

(a) when asked by Hayley; (b) when they noticed she was wriggling; (c) at the normal toileting times.

They also recorded the number of times Hayley was found to be wet.

The tick chart was to be filled in for one week (see p. 71).

Conclusion

Hayley did not ask to use the toilet at all.

The staff noticed Hayley needed the toilet on many occasions.

Hayley used the toilet when taken at the normal times.

Hayley was found to be wet most often after lunch.

Evaluation

Hayley is no longer asking to go to the toilet, which she was able to do three months ago. She appears to have gone backwards in her social training. According to developmental milestones (see Chapter 7, p. 158) the 2½-year-old is 'usually dry in the day'. Hayley was operating at that level in January.

Recommendations

Discuss the problem with Hayley's mother to see if she is able to make her needs known at home.

If there is also a problem at home ask the doctor to investigate a possible urinary tract infection.

If the problem only occurs at nursery, encourage Hayley to ask for the toilet by rewarding her with a star chart.

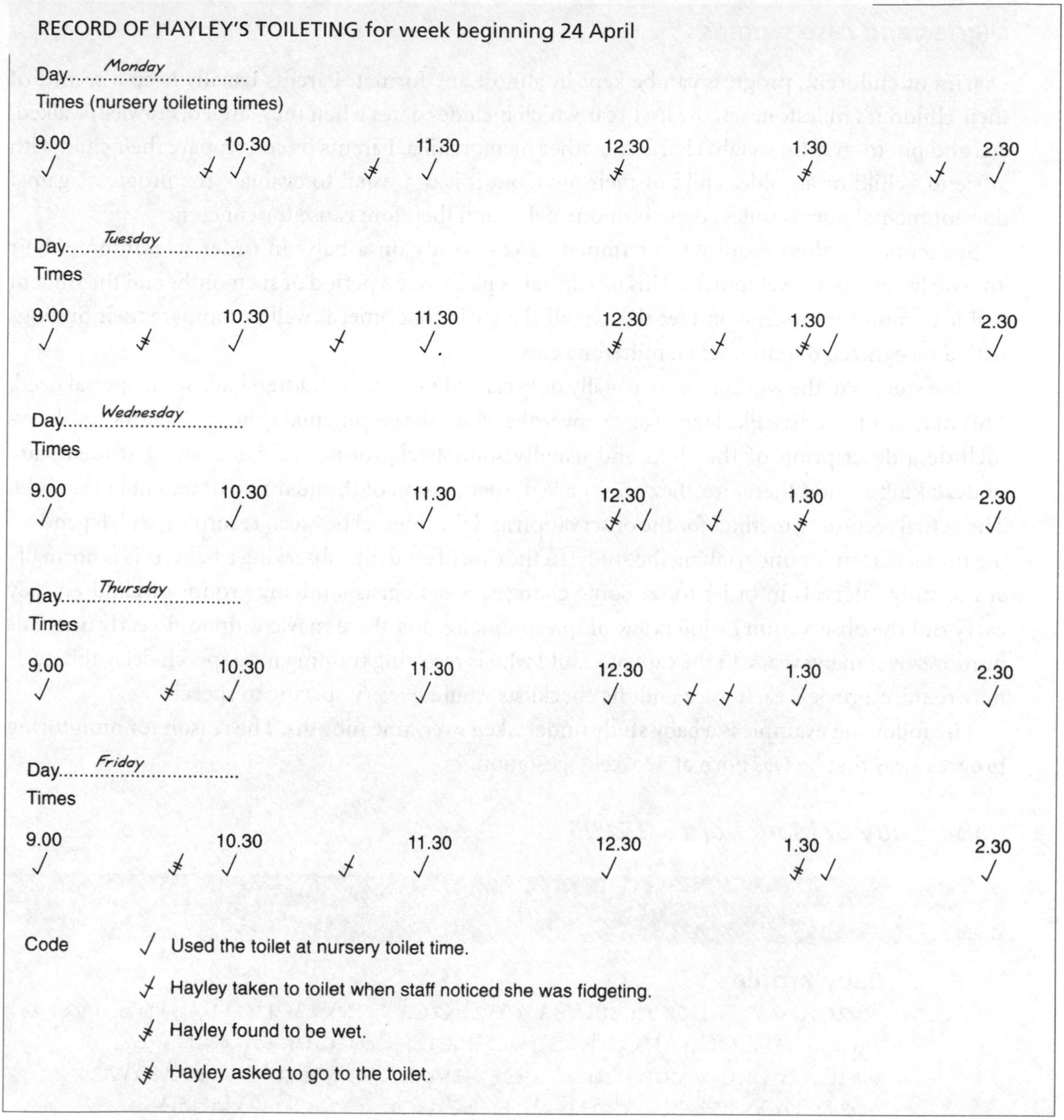

RECORD OF HAYLEY'S TOILETING for week beginning 24 April

Day.......... *Monday*

Times (nursery toileting times)

9.00	10.30	11.30	12.30	1.30	2.30
✓	✗ ✓	✗ ✓	✗	✗	✗ ✓

Day.......... *Tuesday*

Times

9.00	10.30	11.30	12.30	1.30	2.30
✓	✗ ✓	✗ ✓.	✗	✗ ✓	✓

Day.......... *Wednesday*

Times

9.00	10.30	11.30	12.30	1.30	2.30
✓	✓	✓	✗ ✓ ✗	✗	✓

Day.......... *Thursday*

Times

9.00	10.30	11.30	12.30	1.30	2.30
✓	✗ ✓	✓	✓ ✗ ✗	✓	✓

Day.......... *Friday*

Times

9.00	10.30	11.30	12.30	1.30	2.30
✓	✗ ✓	✗ ✓	✓	✗ ✓	✓

Code		
✓	Used the toilet at nursery toilet time.
✗	Hayley taken to toilet when staff noticed she was fidgeting.
✗	Hayley found to be wet.
✗	Hayley asked to go to the toilet.

Figure 3.8 Record of Hayley's toileting

Diaries and case studies

Diaries of children's progress can be kept in almost any format. Parents usually keep a record of their children's milestones in the first year which includes dates when they smiled, crawled, walked, etc. and photo-graphs, weight charts and other memorabilia. Parents often compare their child with a friend's child or an older child of their own, but it is not usual to evaluate the progress against developmental norms unless there is undue delay, and therefore cause for concern.

Students are often required to complete a case study on a baby in order to reinforce their knowledge of child development. This usually takes place over a period of six months and the student is able to monitor progress and see the overall change in that time, as well as compare their findings with a recognized developmental milestone checklist.

Case studies in the workplace are usually only carried out when children have some special need. This may be in one area like language, or cover the whole developmental sphere. Case studies always include a description of the child and usually some background information. If students are undertaking a study, therefore, they must have the permission of the guardian or parent of the child. The actual recording method for the observation and the interval between recording will depend on the initial reason for undertaking the study. In the case of students observing a baby, this is normally at monthly intervals in order to see some changes. Sociologists studying groups of children may carry out the observation by interview or questionnaire, and these may continue at yearly intervals or more, over many years. In the case of a child who is receiving training for a speech delay the study may require a review each week and the checklists would be very specific to speech.

The following example is a baby study undertaken over nine months. The reason for monitoring progress was that he was born at 32 weeks' gestation.

Baby study of Mark born 6.8.2005

Observation

Baby profile

Mark was born at St Michael's Maternity Hospital 6 August 2005. Mark's mother, Caroline, was 32 weeks pregnant and her expected date of delivery was 1 October. Until the beginning of August Caroline had had a normal pregnancy. She was monitored at the antenatal clinic and as this was her first pregnancy she was booked to be delivered in hospital, with an early discharge if all went well.

On 1 August Caroline woke up with severe pain in her back. She phoned the midwife, who visited and arranged for Caroline to be admitted as she was in the early stage of labour. Caroline was put to bed and given drugs to try to stop the labour.

Caroline continued to have some pain and at 10.00 p.m. on 5 August her waters broke. She was moved to the delivery suite and Mark was born at 3.30 a.m. the following morning. He breathed immediately but his weight was only 1.9 kg so he was transferred to the neonatal unit in an incubator.

Caroline made a good recovery and was discharged five days later. She lived fairly close to the hospital so she stayed with Mark during the day, but went home at night. She expressed her breast milk for Mark as he was being tube-fed.

After an initial weight loss Mark started to gain from day 7. He was still being tube-fed as he was unable to suck and he was continuing to be nursed in oxygen in the incubator.

On day 14 Mark stopped breathing. He was resuscitated but it was discovered that his lungs had collapsed. The cause was not known but Mark needed to be put on a ventilator. He was given antibiotics as a precaution.

Mark breathed for himself after five days but he had two more episodes when he had to go back onto the ventilator. Some worries were expressed about the long-term effects of the pressure to his lungs. On 17 September, when Mark was 6 weeks old, he was transferred to a cot and Caroline breast-fed for the first time. Mark tired easily and needed to be tube-fed on occasion but he gained weight and was discharged home on 26 September.

First observation

Date 1.10.2005   **Time commenced** 10.30 a.m.
                        Time completed 11.00 a.m.

Name of child Mark   **Age** 8 weeks

Setting At home

Aim To assess Mark's development.

Objective To record a baseline of Mark's developmental stages for a baby study.

Record of assessment

Mark was lying on his back in his cot. His head was in mid-line with his arms outstretched. When lifted out onto the changing mat Mark's head fell back and needed support. The midwife undressed Mark and weighed him - 3.6 kg. The midwife laid him on his stomach and he moved his head round to look at his mother.

Mark started to cry and his mother turned him over and talked to him as she put his clothes back on. Mark quietened and concentrated on his mother's face. Caroline tried an experiment by poking her tongue out and after a moment Mark copied her.

Caroline prepared herself to feed Mark. When he was offered the breast he turned his head and latched onto the nipple quickly. He sucked well for five minutes. He made occasional grunts as he fed and his toes curled in satisfaction. At the end of the feed Mark concentrated on Caroline's face and he smiled when spoken to.

Conclusion

Mark weighed 3.6 kg.

Mark responded to his mother by copying her gestures and smiling.

When laid on his stomach he lifted and turned his head. When he was lifted up his head fell back.

Evaluation

According to the developmental milestones in Chapter 7 Mark's weight is average for a new-born baby. Although he is 8 weeks old his expected birth date was this week. His head lag when lifted out of the cot is also more like that of a new-born than a baby of 8 weeks. However, he is smiling and responding to his mother.

Mark is gestationally a new-born baby but chronologically he is 8 weeks old. His development according to the normal milestones is somewhere in between the two.

Second observation

Date 7.2.2006
commenced 2.15 p.m.

Age 6 months   **Time**

Time completed 2.50 p.m.

Record of observation

Mark was lying on his stomach on the changing mat. He lifted himself up onto his forearms and looked around the room when he heard the noise of his food being mixed in the kitchen. Caroline came into the room and Mark gurgled as she lifted him into the baby relax chair. He sat up quite straight with support. He ate his mashed vegetables before enjoying a breast feed.

At the end of the feed Caroline stood him up on her lap. Mark took his weight on his legs and bounced up and down before snuggling into Caroline's chest. After a few minutes he started to wriggle and Caroline put him down on his stomach on the changing mat again. He pushed up onto his forearms and looked around then started crying. Caroline turned him over and gave him a rattle. He held it for a few seconds before letting it go. He started to cry again so Caroline changed him and put him down for a sleep. He continued to grizzle for a while and then fell asleep.

Conclusion

Mark is able to lift himself up onto his forearms to look around when he is on his stomach.

He is able to sit with support and to support his own weight when held standing.

Mark is not able to roll over or to hold a rattle for long.

He recognizes familiar sounds like lunch being prepared.

Evaluation

According to the milestones in Chapter 7 a 6-month-old baby is able to support their weight when held standing, is able to sit with support and will recognize familiar sounds and react to them. Mark is doing all these things. A 6-month-old can usually push up onto their hands and roll over, and hold a rattle and transfer it to the other hand. Mark is not able to do these yet.

Third observation

Date 5.5.2006 **Age** 9 months **Time commenced** 12.30 p.m.
Time completed 12.50 p.m.

Record of observation

Mark had just woken from his morning sleep. He was sitting up in the cot calling out. When Caroline entered the room he stopped shouting and lifted up his arms to be taken out.

Caroline laid him on the changing mat and took off the wet nappy. Mark wriggled and turned over. Caroline turned him back and gave him a toy duck to hold. Mark looked at it then put it in his mouth. Caroline carried him downstairs and sat him on the floor in front of the television. Mark sat quite well but then he reached out for a toy brick and fell over. He cried to be sat up again.

Caroline sat him in the high chair and gave him a piece of toast. Mark picked it up and began to suck it.

Conclusion

Mark is able to sit himself up and call for attention.

He can roll over and sits quite well unsupported but he falls over when he reaches out for a toy.

He can hold a toy and transfer it from hand to hand and he finger-feeds.

Evaluation

According to developmental milestones the 9-month-old can shout for attention, examine things with the mouth and finger-feed well. Mark is able to do these.

The 9-month-old is also able to sit for long periods and lean forward to reach a toy without overbalancing. Mark is able to sit well but still overbalances when trying to reach a toy.

The 9-month-old can often pull to stand and start to crawl but Mark has not done this yet. He is still a little behind in his milestones according to his chronological age.

Fourth observation

Date 6.8.2006 **Age** First birthday   **Time commenced** 2.30 p.m.
Time completed 3.00 p.m.

Record of observation

Mark was sitting on the floor playing with a wrapped parcel. He was trying to pull the paper off and put it in his mouth. His mum called to him and he turned round to look at her, then crawled over and pulled himself up using her skirt to assist him. He edged sideways along the settee and grabbed hold of a ball. When it fell off the settee he let go and dropped to the floor to crawl after it.

There was a knock at the door and Mark turned round to see who would come in. When his dad came in he squealed with delight and lifted his arms to be picked up. He bounced up and down in his dad's arms and shouted 'da-da-da'.

Caroline moved towards the door and called to Mark. He stopped and turned to look at her.

'Do you want a drink?' she asked.

'Dink,' he said.

Caroline went out and returned with a drink of juice in a feeding cup. Mark took it in both hands and drank it down.

Conclusion

Mark is able to crawl well and pull himself up to stand.

When something falls he watches where it goes and crawls after it.

He vocalizes and tries to copy speech.

He responds to his own name.

He is able to feed himself using a feeding cup.

Evaluation

According to the milestones in Chapter 7 the 1-year-old is crawling, pulling to stand and walking round the furniture. They drop toys and watch them fall then look in the right direction when they roll out of sight. They babble and may say two or three single words. They are able to drink from a cup with a little assistance. Mark is able to do all of these.

Overall evaluation

Mark was born 8 weeks early and had severe breathing problems. He had some developmental delay up to the age of 9 months but he had caught up completely by a year.

Checklists

The example given in Chapter 1 showed a checklist for recording a group of children's physical abilities. The following two examples show how checklists can be used for individual children. The first compares a child's physical development with those set out in a recognized developmental scale and requires you to prepare a list of those norms to be completed. The norms are taken from Mary Sheridan's *From Birth to Five Years* (1997).

The second example looks at one area, concentrating over a fairly short period of time. It requires you to think carefully about what you want to find out and how to set about it. In this example it was decided that recording the amount of time the child was on task/off task would give a good guide as to whether she was interested, and therefore concentrating.

Observation

Checklist using norms of gross motor development according to a recognized source

Date 6.2.2006   **Time commenced** 10.45 a.m.
                                            Time completed 11.45 a.m.

Number of adults 2

Number of children 1

Name of child Georgia   **Age** 3 years 8 months

Aim To observe G's gross motor skills while using soft play equipment.

To see if a 3 year 8 month child meets the 'norms' for her developmental progress.

Objective To use a checklist for gross motor development from a recognized source - From Birth to Five Years by Mary Sheridan (1997).

Setting Sports centre with soft play equipment, climbing frame with things to crawl through, jump through and ropes to walk through. There are other children using the equipment. G will be observed over a period of time in order to complete the tasks.

Record of observation

Activity Age 4 years	Yes	No	Sometimes	Comment
Walks or runs alone up and down stairs, one foot to one step.	Yes			When G walks up steps, she walks up them as an adult would.
Navigates self-locomotion skilfully, turning sharp corners, running, pushing and pulling.	Yes	No		G navigated herself around the room with apparent ease and did not bump into anyone. G was not seen to push or pull during the observation.
Climbs ladders and trees.	Yes	No		Not observed climbing a tree, but she climbed a rope ladder and rope web.
Can stand, walk and run on tiptoe.	Yes			G shows her mother 'fairy runs', she stands on her tiptoes and reaches for a bar.
Sits with knees crossed	Yes			G sat down and crossed her legs.

Activity Age 5 years	Yes	No	Sometimes	Comment
Walks easily on narrow line.	Yes			G uses her arms to balance herself as she walks confidently in a straight line.
Runs lightly on toes.	Yes		Sometimes	G shows her mother 'fairy runs' but does not always run on her toes.
Grips strongly with either hand.	Yes			G hangs from a bar with one hand and makes monkey noises.
Active and skilful in climbing, sliding.	Yes	No		G climbs the climbing frame, slides and attempts cartwheels.

Conclusion

Tassoni et al. (2002, p. 168) state that:

Age 3 years	Age 4 years
'Walks and runs forwards.'	'Runs changing direction.'

From the observation G is able to walk and run forwards, she also changes direction and is successful in navigating herself around a large busy room avoiding obstructions and people.

Page 169:

Age 3 years

'Walks on tiptoes.'

G is able to walk and run on her tiptoes, but she does not do this consistently; she sometimes walks on her feet normally and sometimes runs normally on her feet.

Tassoni et al. (2002) again:

Age 5 years

'Runs quickly and is able to avoid obstacles.'

G ran quickly around the room; she did not collide with anybody or anything.

Age 5 years

'Is able to use a variety of large equipment – e.g. swings, slides.'

G successfully used the slides and large equipment in the room.

Beaver et al. (2001, p. 191) state that:

Age 4 years

'Children are confident at climbing over and through apparatus.'

In the soft play centre G climbed over and through apparatus; she climbed successfully and confidently.

Age 4 years

'She walks or runs up and down stairs, putting one foot on each step.'

G ran up and down steps using one foot on each step (as an adult might). She also walked up and down steps with one foot on each step, but she was not seen walking or running up and down a staircase.

Evaluation

The method used for the observation was a checklist observation. The advantages of undertaking a checklist observation are that they are quick and easy to record, particularly in a public place. One disadvantage of doing a checklist observation is that the information is closed data and the information collected does not necessarily give a holistic picture of the child, but of their performance only at the time the observation was undertaken.

However, the method of observation was effective in meeting its aims.

According to Bruce and Meggitt (2002, p. 135), the developmental norms of a 3-year-old are that:

'The child can jump from a low step.

She walks backwards and sideways.

She can stand and walk on tiptoe and stand on one foot.

She has good spatial awareness.

She rides a tricycle using the pedals.

She can climb stairs with one foot on each step – downwards with two feet per step.'

Age 4 years

'Sense of balance is developing; she may be able to walk along a line. She enjoys climbing trees and on frames, she can run up and down stairs, one foot per step.'

Page 236:

Age 5 years

'The child can use a variety of play equipment – slides, swings, climbing frames.

She can play ball games.

She can hop and run lightly on her toes and move rhythmically to music.

Her sense of balance is well developed.'

From the observation it is evident that G is a physically able and active child. G is reaching all of the developmental norms of her age group and is also achieving some of the developmental norms of a 4-year-old and even some of the developmental skills of a 5-year-old.

A.H. Maslow had a theory of developmental needs: Maslow's hierarchy of needs. Physical play and activity are two of the lowest level needs. Children need the physiological needs to be met before they can move on to the higher level needs. Once G's physical needs are met, she can then progress to the next level - safety needs: hygiene, security, protection and shelter.

Recommendations

In order for G's needs to be met, an adult should support the child's learning. In the UK, the Effective Early Learning Project has identified three main ways in which adults can help support children to learn and achieve. Pascal and Bertram in Curtis and O'Hagan (2003) named this the 'Engagement Scale':

It considers:

- how the adult encourages the child to achieve independence
- the sensitivity of the adult to the child
- how the adult offers stimulating and challenging experiences.

(Curtis and O'Hagan 2003, p. 155)

A further recommendation would be for G to have more opportunities to play and socialize with children of her own age and a little older. By interacting with other children in a physically stimulating environment G will benefit from having the support of and fun with her friends. G would also benefit from joining a gymnastics club, which would encourage her to learn new skills such as balancing on a beam and moving around in different ways. Joining a physically challenging group would enable G to continue developing physically and help her to become strong, with better self-esteem. G would also be keeping fit and healthy by having fun. A swimming class could also benefit G, which may give her confidence and also raise her self-esteem.

Curtis and O'Hagan (2003, p. 162) say: 'it is essential that children at the Foundation Stage get as many opportunities as possible for physical exercise as it is vital for their later academic development.'

Observation

Checklist – pre-coded for time and concentration on task

Date   18.5.2006

Number of adults 1   **Time commenced** 12.50 p.m.

Number of children 4   **Time completed** 1.05 p.m.

Name of child Karla   **Age** 4 years 6 months

Aim   To observe a group of children, and in particular one child, to record how long she spent on task and engrossed in what she was doing.

Objective To see how a 4½-year-old concentrates on what she is doing, and how co-operatively the children play without any adult intervention.

Setting A table-top game of Racing Snails being played with board and dice by four children in a nursery.

Record of observation

Time	On task – engrossed	On task – not engrossed	Off task – quiet	Off task – disruptive
12.50	✓			
12.51			✓	
12.52			✓	
12.53	✓			
12.54			✓	
12.55	✓			
12.56			✓	
12.57	✓			
12.58			✓	
12.59	✓			
1.00			✓	
1.01	✓			
1.02	✓			
1.03			✓	
1.04	✓			

Conclusion

The game lasted for 15 minutes and there was a lot of co-operation by all of the participants. There was good evidence of socialization and use of language (although this is not evident from the recording of the observation). Children took turns with the dice and moved the snails in the proper way for most of the time.

Evaluation

Karla concentrated for the majority of the time that the game was being played. She co-operated well with the group of children, which is typical for a 4-year-old (see Chapter 7). She was able to take turns and to approach the game in a reasonable manner. Her concentration span was good compared with some of the other children.

Recommendations

Karla's concentration span was good, so more pre-reading and pre-writing activities could be encouraged so as to maintain this level of concentration, and prepare her for school next term.

The method used was suitable to record concentration span and enabled the recorder to demonstrate this. However, it would be possible to undertake an observation of the same activity to find out different aspects of the child's development. As noted in the conclusion, a lot of language took place which was not obvious in the chart. There was an occasional dispute about the number of moves to be made or the number thrown on the dice. This did not essentially interrupt the game but would identify another aspect of the children's developmental stage. It is important therefore to consider the method and aims carefully before undertaking an observation.

Observations Using Other Media for Recording

Figure 3.2 (p. 42) showed various media for recording your observations. We have demonstrated the use of graphs (block), diagrams (tracking) and written material. It is not possible to show you the use of tape and video but do try if you have the opportunity. They enable you to record longer periods in detail and you can repeatedly play them back in order to make your evaluations. Tape is obviously very useful for looking at language and children's understanding of why things happen, e.g. using it to record their ideas about where rain comes from. You might need to practise to enable the children to get used to working with tape. Do remember that the recorder will pick up all the surrounding noise, so choose somewhere quiet.

The last observation uses a photograph and a copy of the child's work to record the results. It would require the permission of the parent if you intended to use it as part of your portfolio, as the photo would mean the child is identifiable. Using the children's work as evidence is very useful for some types of observation, especially those assessing intellectual/cognitive skills.

Observation

Date 27.3.2006

Time commenced 2.15 p.m.
Time completed 2.35 p.m.

Name of child Billy

Age 6 years 3 months

Setting The construction area of a Year 1 classroom during a free-play session.

Aim To discover a 6-year-old's ability to draw what he sees.

Objective To observe and record a child's ability to draw a representation of a construction he built using wooden bricks.

Record of observation
Billy has been carefully constructing a building using a selection of wooden bricks of various shapes. He works alongside a small group of other children, but he does not communicate with them as he is concentrating on what he is building. When he completes the task I ask him if it would be possible to draw a picture of the castle so it could be kept as a record of his building. Billy answers, 'Yes, it is a castle with a drawbridge and a moat, there are gaps for the arrows to be fired

through by the keep.' As he draws the representation of the castle Billy comments that 'the drawbridge will be pulled up if the enemy attacks the castle - it is a medieval castle with a lot of fortifications'. It takes a few more minutes for Billy to complete his picture.

Figure 3.9 Billy with his model and his drawing

Conclusion

As the photograph shows, Billy was able to make a good attempt at recording the building in some detail. He noticed where the different shapes were in relation to each other and had the sizes quite well in proportion.

Evaluation

Billy demonstrated that he could 'draw more realistic and complicated pictures', one of the developmental milestones for a 6-year-old (see Chapter 7). His use of language indicates a widening of vocabulary and the ability to talk confidently and fluently.

You have now had the opportunity to read examples of the various types of observation you can use to record and evaluate children's behaviour.

However, at times there could be some limiting factors when undertaking observations. Factors that could be affecting children on the day of the observation may include the following:

- The child may be unhappy and/or be worried about something in their home life.
- Weather conditions may affect where the observation is to take place – it could be too hot/sunny, wet/raining or cold/snowy – thus preventing outdoor play or affecting conditions indoors adversely.
- Is the classroom conducive to undertaking an observation – is it too noisy/busy or are there any interruptions or disruptive factors?
- The child may be unwell, or have just returned to nursery/school following an absence through illness.
- The child might be hungry or tired.
- The child may simply not be interested in completing a task at that time.

When recording or evaluating an observation it is important to include aspects that have been given consideration which might have affected the outcome. It is also important to remember that all observation methods have limitations, for example a checklist may have insufficient detail, and this should also be noted.

There now follow some suggestions for Aims and Objectives that you might like to use to practise the skill for yourself. First, decide which method you think will give you the best result. There are no 'right' answers; you should try them out and see. If you find one method unsuitable then try another.

Remember, observations need to include the following details, which will demonstrate your knowledge and understanding of how to meet the individual needs of the child/children:

- date and immediate environment for the observation;
- clear aims and objectives for the observation;
- maintenance of confidentiality;
- records of the observation presented clearly and appropriately;
- appropriate conclusions which include information that links to the following:
  - ages and stages of development
  - child development theory or norm where appropriate;
- evaluation of the results of your observation in relation to identified theories or norms of child development;
- a description of how you would promote the child's development as a result of the observation, giving practical suggestions;
- an explanation of how these can be implemented;
- evidence of an understanding of anti-discriminatory/anti-bias practice where appropriate.

Suggestions for Aims and Objectives

1. AIM: To observe the physical ability of a 7-month-old baby.
   OBJECTIVE: To watch movement from the supine to prone position and to observe the head, shoulder and neck movements.
2. AIM: To observe the balance and movement of a 9-month-old baby.
   OBJECTIVE: To watch how a 9-month-old can reach the sitting position without help and how they can sit without support for a considerable time.

3. AIM: To observe the hand–eye co-ordination and fine motor skills of a 2-year-old.
   OBJECTIVE: To look at the ability of a 2-year-old to guide hand movements with the eyes and see if a preferred hand is used.
4. AIM: To observe a new entrant.
   OBJECTIVE: To watch how the child integrates and socializes with the other children and to identify what helps the child settle into the new group.
5. AIM: To observe a 4-year-old's language development.
   OBJECTIVE: To observe the vocabulary, the conversational ability and the questioning that a 4-year-old is using.
6. AIM: To observe a 5-year-old's social development.
   OBJECTIVE: To observe a 5-year-old's ability to relate to adults and to integrate with small and large groups of children.
7. AIM: To observe why children are attracted to an activity in the nursery setting.
   OBJECTIVE: To see what initially attracts the child, what keeps them at the activity and whether the activity has a satisfactory outcome.
8. AIM: To observe a 4-year-old during a free-choice session.
   OBJECTIVE: To note the choice of activities and observe the length of concentration on each activity.
9. AIM: To observe a group of 4-year-olds in the home corner.
   OBJECTIVE: To see if children interact and engage in elaborate and prolonged imaginative play.
10. AIM: To observe a small group of 5-year-olds playing with clay.
    OBJECTIVE: To observe and record the manipulative skills and the imagination of 5-year-olds while playing with this tactile material.
11. AIM: To observe a 5-year-old during an outdoor play session.
    OBJECTIVE: To observe and record whether they are able to run, skip, climb, jump, and throw and catch a ball and are agile and energetic.
12. AIM: To observe a 3-year-old painting.
    OBJECTIVE: To see and record how the child experiments with the paint and brush.
13. AIM: To observe the interaction between two boys of similar age (7) while playing with a construction set.
    OBJECTIVE: To see how the boys co-operate in the task and record the language they use.
14. AIM: To observe the gross motor skills of a class of 4-year-olds.
    OBJECTIVE: To record their ability to balance, climb and control a ball.
15. AIM: To observe the social skills of a 3-month-old baby.
    OBJECTIVE: To identify how a young baby communicates before language emerges, and how they show pleasure by facial expressions.
16. AIM: To identify how a 6-month-old baby spends a day.
    OBJECTIVE: To record what proportion of the day is spent awake, asleep, crying, feeding, playing, etc.
17. AIM: To observe a group of 10-year-olds participating in a science experiment.
    OBJECTIVE: To watch the group and identify their level of skill in observing, analysing, concluding and predicting the results of an experiment.
18. AIM: To observe a 13-year-old using equipment in the adventure playground.
    OBJECTIVE: To track the choice of equipment used.
    To observe how equipment is used.
19. AIM: To observe how a group of children use a small-scale train set.
    OBJECTIVE: To observe and record imaginative play, co-operative play and language used.

20. AIM: To observe a 5-year-old during free play.

OBJECTIVE: To observe their concentration span in different activities.

21. AIM: To observe a group of 4-year-old children in the role-play area.

OBJECTIVE: To see if children interact and engage in elaborate and prolonged imaginative play.
To record language used.

22. AIM: To observe their 11-year-old completing a drawing of their friend.

OBJECTIVE: To see if they observe before drawing.

To see if they have a sense of proportion.

To see if there is a reasonable likeness.

23. AIM: To observe a group of 14-year-olds planning a short play during literacy.

OBJECTIVE: To identify their ability to work together to plan and compromise if necessary.

To identify if all the group take part, or leaders emerge.

To identify if they can keep to time and complete the task.

24. AIM: To observe a 5-year-old's social skill at lunchtime.

OBJECTIVE: To identify the child's ability to respond to others and to use cutlery effectively.

REFERENCES

Beaver, M., Brewster, J., Jones, P., Neaum, S. and Tallack, J. (2001) *Babies and Young Children: Diploma in Childcare and Education.* Cheltenham: Nelson Thorne.

Bruce, T. and Meggitt, M. (2002) *Child Care and Education* (3rd edn). London: Hodder.

Curtis, A. and O'Hagan, M. (2003) *Care and Education in Early Childhood: A Student's Guide to Theory and Practice.* London: Routledge.

DfEE (1999) *The National Curriculum.* London: DfEE/QCA.

Geraghty, P. (1988) *Caring for Children* (2nd edn). London: Bailliere Tindall.

Greydanus, D. (1997) *Caring for Your Adolescent.* Oxford: Oxford University Press.

Lee, C. (1990) *Growth and Development of Children* (4th edn). Harlow: Longman.

National Council for Curriculum and Assessment, Republic of Ireland.
http://www.scotland.gov.uk/Topics/Education/Schools/curriculum (accessed 11 August 2006).

Reynolds, V. (1994) *A Practical Guide to Child Development, Vol. 1: The Child.* Cheltenham: Thorne.

Scottish Executive, Curriculum and Assessment. http://www.scotland.gov.uk/Topics/Education/Schools/curriculum (accessed 11 August 2006).

Sheridan, M. (1997) *From Birth to Five Years.* London: NFER.

Sheridan, M. (1975) *Developmental Progress of Infants and Young Children.* HMSO (3rd edn).

Tassoni, P., Beith, K., Eldridge, H. and Gough, A. (2002) *Diploma: Child Care and Education.* Oxford: Heinemann.

CHAPTER FOUR

Extending and Utilizing Your Observations

At the end of this chapter you will be able to:

- **Observe and record in increased detail.**

- **Understand why your observations are important to the children in your care.**

- **Recognize the need to work with others to achieve your aims.**

- **Understand the roles and responsibilities of professionals working with children.**

By the end of the previous chapter you should have been able to satisfy yourself that the observations you have completed conform to three main criteria:

1 You have observed children carefully enough and for sufficient time to see what they are capable of. This may mean observing on more than one occasion or using different methods.

2 You have read widely and understand why children behave in the ways that they do. You know the normal developmental stages.

3 You have used your knowledge to plan activities and routines which will encourage children to move forward. These are challenging enough to enable the children to feel a sense of achievement, but are not beyond the children's ability.

Once you are well practised in observation you will find that you tend to assess children throughout your working day. These assessments help with planning, but we can still make assumptions about a child because we only notice them at certain times. If we do not take the time to make detailed observations we may miss important facts.

As Joan Tough (1976) found when talking to teachers about their class, one commented, 'I haven't any quiet ones, I wish I had, all my children talk all the time.' Among those children on whom she ran a sampling check was Sheila, and these were the teacher's comments after observation:

> Sheila's not very big for her age and I think I must have overlooked her before. She gave an answer when I spoke to her, just a short one, but I couldn't tell what she said. I never saw her speak to anyone else and much of the time she was on her own, playing with

jigsaws or pegboard. In fact, she never moved from the table until playtime. I think she needs help trying out other things and in approaching other children and I must find out what her speech difficulties are. (p. 47)

This observation was undertaken in a reception class. The teacher understood that Sheila's behaviour was not what is expected for the age group.

How do you know what to expect a child will be able to do?

You will learn from working with children as well as from research and development charts. You need to know what to expect so that you can advise parents or refer the child for more specialist assessment. Take speech, for example. A child of 30 months has joined your nursery and his only words are 'mum', 'dad', 'ball'. The parents want to know if this small vocabulary is normal for this age.

You cannot answer if you have no idea of normal speech development. As Harold Fishbein (1984, p. 7) noted:

> As soon as we can describe a developmental sequence and locate a child on that sequence we can begin to make some reasonable judgements about his rate of development, whether behind or ahead of other children, and to make some predictions as to what to expect next.

Language is important as it is often linked to ability:

> Until the child can express his ideas, intentions and needs through the use of language, other people can only guess what it is he wants them to know from his gestures and actions, from the tone of his voice and from his facial expression. (Tough, 1976, p. 8)

On the other hand, if you are aware of what is normal, you can reassure parents who may feel there is a problem when their children use language that is not Standard English. As Julia Berryman (2002) reminds us: 'Young children by the age of 3–4 often produce sentences containing the regularised form of irregular words.' Examples of this would be: 'I digged in the garden', 'We holded the kittens', 'The sheeps runned away'.

Language relates not only to the number of words a child can use but also to how much a child understands of what is being said. We cannot gain a true picture of a child's ability unless they have the opportunity to demonstrate what they are capable of. We need to be aware of the cultural, social, emotional and physical factors which may affect our evaluation. Indeed, Margaret Donaldson believes that 'failure is a perverse inability of the teacher and student to come to terms with the communication problem' (Bruner, in Foreword of Grieve and Hughes, 1990).

This is not usually a conscious decision, but as children grow older we begin to rely heavily on an understanding of language, both spoken and written, in order to evaluate progress. Many people who did not have their dyslexia recognized have testified to the trauma this caused in their lives. In a discussion of writing, Miranda Jones (in Grieve and Hughes, 1990) comments:

> The importance which society places on literacy and logic means that children who find it difficult to learn are quickly made to feel inadequate. The teacher's task, therefore, is to build on what the child has already discovered about reading and writing. Obviously this will be facilitated by knowing what sort of a knowledge base is already in existence.

This is why a thorough assessment using developmental checklists (see Chapter 7) and detailed observation is so important. Observations should become 'records of achievement' with recommendations for targets for further achievement.

Consider the following situation:

Mrs Wallace brings her daughter Sophie (3 years and 4 months) to your nursery for a visit. The family has recently moved into the area after living abroad for 2 years. Sophie has not attended a nursery before and her mother is quite anxious about how she will settle. She stays for about an hour with her mother and does not attempt to move away from her. When approached by staff she hides her head. A further visit is arranged and this follows a similar pattern. After discussion between the manager and Mrs Wallace it is decided that Sophie will come to the nursery on three mornings a week. When asked if Sophie has any special name for the toilet, drink, etc. so staff will know what she wants, Mrs Wallace replies 'No'.

Sophie is brought to the nursery by her father, who says that his wife can't face having to leave her and see her possibly upset. You help Sophie to take her coat off and stay with her for the morning. After talking to the manager Mr Wallace says goodbye and leaves. Sophie looks at her dad leaving and begins to cry quietly. You take her over to a table where a group of children are doing puzzles and let her sit on your lap while you start to do a puzzle. You ask Sophie if she would like to help but she does not respond. After a few minutes she stops crying but still shows no sign of wanting to join in. You take her round the nursery to look at the various areas to see if she appears to be interested in anything but she clings to you. Most of the children want to play outside before snack time so you put Sophie's coat on and show her the bikes, cars and prams. She takes hold of a pram but another child comes rushing by on a bike, so she grips your hand again and stays by your side for the rest of the session. At snack time Sophie is offered milk and juice; she points to the juice. After snack time the children sit on the mat to listen to a story. Sophie sits quietly and appears to be listening but she does not respond to any of the questions. At the end of the morning, when her mother comes to collect her, she smiles and runs over to her.

A pattern develops over the next few sessions. Sophie cries initially but this doesn't last long. She stays fairly close to you and will sit drawing or completing a jigsaw. She responds to questioning with nods or pointing. She watches other children playing but does not attempt to join in. She seems to dislike loud noise. If she needs something, such as going to the toilet, she pulls you towards the door.

At first you attribute this behaviour to the fact that Sophie is shy. She is an only child who has not been used to mixing and being separated from her mother, but as time goes by you begin to wonder if something is wrong.

What should you do?

First, raise your concerns at the staff meeting: have others noticed the same pattern of behaviour? Your manager will then probably suggest that you carry out an observation before she discusses Sophie with her parents.

What are your main concerns?

You may decide that you are interested in finding out whether Sophie makes any attempt to talk to staff or children during her time at the nursery. You may want to see if she tries to join in any activity involving other children.

How are you going to find this out, remembering that you want to give Sophie the best possible chance to give a true picture of her ability?

Activity

Look at page 56. If you agree that time sampling is a possible solution, write out your Aim and Objectives. Then decide how often you need to observe and over what time period.

If your observation or observations confirm that Sophie does not attempt to play with other children and does not talk to anyone in the nursery, then you need to consider whether this is what you expect of a child of her age.

How are you going to do that?

You can compare her behaviour with that of other children of the same age in the nursery. You also need to read about the social and language skills of 3½-year-old children. The fact that you noticed her behaviour suggests that she was not behaving like the other children of similar age. Developmental charts show that a 3-year-old has 'Extensive vocabulary that is usually intelligible even to strangers', and 'Begins to join in games with other children and to share, but still needs to be in small groups'. (See Chapter 7 on developmental milestones.)

You need to understand how speech and social skills develop in order to suggest further investigation and action planning.

Remember, Plan and Carry Out Activity + Observation + Evaluation = Action

Joan Tough, in *Listening to Children Talking* (1976), has a chapter on 'The child who does not talk'. Although the research was carried out over 30 years ago, many of her findings are relevant today. Three main reasons for lack of speech are generally accepted: physical abnormality, lack of stimulation and emotional problems. Joan Tough used extensive observation as an assessment tool but also commented that it is vital to talk to the family to gain a fuller picture. In this instance it would be very important to arrange an interview with Mr and Mrs Wallace to see if Sophie talks at home and to find out what opportunities she has had for playing with other children. This meeting would probably be set up by your manager, but you might be asked to attend as you are the person who has had the most contact with Sophie.

At the interview Mr Wallace admits that he has not spent a great deal of time with Sophie. His job involves long hours and she is often in bed when he comes home. Mrs Wallace is a very quiet person herself and when she lived abroad had not felt very confident about going out when she did not speak the language well. She and Sophie spent a lot of time together drawing, cooking and playing games but she realizes that they did not do much singing or talking about what was going on as this seemed rather a strange thing to do on your own with a child. Sophie had not been to the local kindergarten as there were no other English-speaking children in the area. Both parents were reasonably happy with Sophie's behaviour. She had walked at a year, was toilet trained by 18 months and she seemed to understand when asked to do something. They admitted that she only used a very occasional word, relying on the fact that they understood her gestures.

How would you expect your manager to proceed?

It appears that Sophie is a much-loved child but that she may not have been spoken to very much. She has not had the opportunity to mix with other children. Her physical and cognitive development are within normal limits. Her drawing suggests that she is even a little ahead.

One possibility which should occur to you is that Sophie may have some degree of hearing loss. The family has been living abroad so she may not have been monitored by the Health Visitor on a regular basis. Mrs Wallace says that a doctor was available for staff and their families. Sophie had her immunizations but she had not had any screening tests. The family has just registered with the GP so it was suggested that an appointment with the Health Visitor would be a good idea. If it was found that Sophie had hearing loss and no specific reason such as an infection was detected, the Health Visitor would probably refer her for a more exact test with the audiologist. It would also be a good idea to make a referral to the speech therapist as these appointments often take quite a long time to come through. (See pp. 109–11 for descriptions of professional roles.)

A hearing loss is often the reason why a child fails to talk, but if you have read widely you will also realize that 'Pre-school language impairment, or the late acquisition of speech, are important and useful early indicators of dyslexia' (Ott, 1997).

There are several other indicators and the speech therapist or educational psychologist will take a careful history before making a diagnosis. It will not be up to you or your manager to make these decisions, but as you can see it was your observation which led to the matter being investigated. Hopefully there will not be a long-term problem, but the longer it is left the more likely it is that the problem will intensify. In the meantime you should be planning activities to encourage sounds and speech, and making sure that you:

- Look at Sophie when you talk.
- Use gestures to reinforce your instructions.
- Name objects as you play with them.
- Encourage interaction in small groups without too much distraction.
- Praise and encourage any attempts to interact with other children or make sounds.

You then need to continue to observe and record her achievements. This becomes a planning cycle.

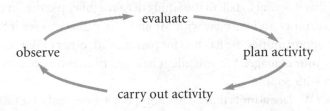

This cycle is important for all children, but especially so for those with a special need. Observation is the only way to know if a plan of action is successful or if changes are necessary.

The next two observations demonstrate how two children (Colin and Ryan) with apparently similar problems – an inability to act in ways socially and emotionally appropriate for their age – actually have very different problems and require different action plans.

Colin (3 years, 10 months) used to enjoy coming to nursery but lately has become very tearful and angry when his mother leaves. He refuses to join in games and throws himself to the floor when asked to join in the singing or go outside on the big toys. His spoken language is excellent, his drawing detailed and he can recognize several words. It is decided to observe Colin by time sampling over a period of an hour each morning for four mornings to see if anything is triggering the behaviour.

Observation

Day 1

09.00 Colin is brought to nursery by his mother. He tugs her back towards the door shouting 'No, no'. Mother tries to reason with him and asks him to take his coat off. He pulls it more closely round him and continues to scream. Mother is becoming more agitated so a nursery nurse takes hold of him, and suggests his mother says goodbye and leaves. Colin kicks the nursery nurse as she tries to restrain him from running out of the door after his mother.

09.10 The children are sitting on the mat for registration. Colin is sitting with the nursery nurse looking at a book. He points to words, asking 'What does that say?' When asked to be quiet to listen for his name, he throws the book, hitting one of the other children. The nursery nurse asks him to say sorry but he looks away and refuses.

09.20 The children have been asked to choose what they plan to do this morning. Colin is sitting in the writing area. He is absorbed in the activity, and when asked what he is doing he looks quite indignant before answering 'I'm writing a letter to my grandma.'

09.30 Colin is still in the writing area. He is reading the letter back to himself. He appears satisfied with his work. He asks for an envelope to put it in.

09.40 Colin has moved into the book corner. He has arranged several of the soft toys in a row, and is reading a story to them. His voice goes up and down as he assumes the different characters in Goldilocks and the Three Bears.

09.50 Colin is still in the book corner. The children have been asked to start clearing away but Colin makes no attempt to put his book down. Another child comes over and starts to put the toys back on the shelf. Colin looks up and sees what is happening. He shouts, 'No, don't do that, they are listening to a story.' When the child says it is clearing-up time, he grabs the teddy bear she is holding and attempts to take it back. When she holds on he bends over to bite. (Observation suspended as you intervene.)

Day 2

09.00   Colin is brought to nursery by his grandmother. He is sullen when left, but does not scream. He takes his coat off and sits hunched up in the book corner. When approached by other children he puts his foot out to try to trip them. They move away and sit on the mat.

09.10   At registration Colin is still sitting in the corner. A nursery nurse sits beside him and tries to encourage him to move closer to the group. He ignores her. When asked what he plans to do this morning, he chooses the writing area.

09.20   Colin is sitting in the writing area looking into space. When asked what he wants to do, he says he is thinking up a story to write. He has folded some pieces of paper up to resemble a book.

09.30   Colin is engrossed in writing his story. Two other children have moved into the area but he ignores them. A child leans across the table to put a colouring pencil back into the pot. He accidentally makes a mark on Colin's page, which sends him into a rage. He stamps, shouts, 'You've ruined it', and proceeds to tear the book up. The other child looks startled and begins to cry. A nursery nurse assures him it was an accident. She suggests Colin might like to try something else. He stamps out of the area and goes over to the home corner. He throws the bedding from the cot onto the floor and then sits under the table.

09.40   Colin is still under the table. He refuses to pick up the bedding.

09.50   Colin is still under the table. Attempts to coax him out have all failed. It is now tidy-up time and the other children tidy up around him. (It is decided to ignore Colin while continuing to observe.)

10.00   Colin has moved out from under the table. He has taken out a jigsaw puzzle and put it on the table. The other children are sitting on the floor holding what they have made, painted, etc., ready to tell the rest of the group what they have been doing. The nursery nurse asks Colin to come and sit down. He ignores her so one of the staff takes him by the hand and sits with him. When he is asked what he has done this morning, he says he wrote a story 'but it got ruined'.

Day 3

You are beginning to realize that Colin's behaviour seems to be linked to interruptions when he is absorbed in an activity. He also appears to stay on his own for most of the time.

To find out if this is the case you decide to observe for the whole morning.

To make recording easier you monitor Colin at fifteen-minute intervals using the following headings.

Time	Activity	Interactions
09.15	Colin arrives late with mother. She explains he had a temper tantrum.	Refuses to speak to anyone.
09.30	Doing some colouring, being very careful not to go over the lines.	Chatting to nursery nurse about a visit to the zoo.
09.45	'Writing' about the zoo visit.	None.
10.00	Sitting on the mat with other children, telling the nursery nurse about his story.	Gives a very full explanation of what he had been writing.

10.15	Having juice and a biscuit at the table.	None.
10.30	The children have gone outside to play. Colin is beside the wall. He is scowling and occasionally kicks the wall.	Muttering under his breath.
10.45	Takes off coat and hangs it up. Hurries over to the table and sits down with his group. Looks at the picture of the Three Billy Goats on his worksheet. When the nursery nurse (N.N.) asks if anyone knows which is the smallest he puts up his hand and is picked to answer. 'This is the smallest, this is the middle-sized and this is the biggest. He isn't frightened by the Troll.'	Smiles at nursery nurse.
11.00	Colin is drawing his version of the story.	Talking to N.N.
11.15	The children are singing nursery rhymes. Colin is being calmed down after an outburst.	Shouting 'I want to go.'
11.30	Sitting listening to a story tape.	None.
11.45	Wandering around the nursery while the others are collecting their work to take home.	
12.00	Collected by mother.	Chats away about the story when asked what he did.

Colin's mother is aware that he has been observed and is anxious to discuss his problem. He does not have similar outbursts at home. He has two older sisters and appears to relate well to them. A meeting is arranged for the following morning.

Day 4

Colin arrives at the nursery in a rage. He is shouting 'I told you I didn't want to come. I don't want to play. I want to work.'

He and his mother are invited into the office and the manager waits for Colin to calm down. She then asks him if he can explain why he doesn't like coming to nursery. He replies that he doesn't like playing, he wants to do work. When asked 'What work?', he replies 'Reading and writing and the computer'. The manager asks if he would like to do some work now and he agrees. This allows the discussion to go on without Colin. Mrs Edwards is asked about the sort of things Colin does at home. It becomes apparent that he is very involved with language activities and has a lot of 'educational' toys. His father spends time helping him play word and number-matching games on the computer and his older sisters also encourage him.

Evaluation

When this information is added to the behaviour observed at the nursery it becomes very clear that Colin is frustrated if he is unable to complete a task. It also confirms that he is not very good at socializing with his peer group. His cognitive development is well advanced, but he is likely to experience difficulty at school if his social and emotional problems are not addressed.

With this knowledge it is now possible to plan with his mother. Perhaps he could have a friend to tea or go on an outing with the family. In the nursery Colin will still be encouraged to do the activities he enjoys, but he will be warned when only 5 minutes are left so that he can plan to finish. At the computer he might be able to help another child.

Children who are naturally shy or prefer to work on their own will not change dramatically, but they can learn how to co-operate with others, and to experience some of the pleasures of shared activities.

The second observation is of Ryan, who has just had his fourth birthday. Ryan has poor speech. It is difficult to understand what he says and he does not use sentences. He can be very disruptive and often finds himself in trouble. It is decided to shadow him for a whole morning. This takes up all the time for one member of staff, but it is hoped to discover more about why Ryan has problems with the rest of the group.

Observation

09.00   Ryan bursts into the nursery and runs through to the coat area. He pulls off his coat and throws it onto the peg. It misses and falls on the floor. A nursery nurse asks him to pick it up, but he has gone. He goes into the main nursery and selects a plastic giraffe from the shelf which he plays with, making it walk along the table.

09.10   The nursery nurse is sitting in the book area with the rest of the children. 'Come and sit down for registration, Ryan.' Ryan continues to play with the giraffe, so she stands up and reaches over to take his hand. Ryan struggles and pulls away. He hides under a table and begins to 'eat' the giraffe. He is ignored for a while but then another member of staff takes the giraffe away and sits him on her lap. He remains seated sucking his thumb. The group are deciding where they would like to work first this morning. 'Where are you going to choose, Ryan?' Without removing his thumb, he mumbles something. 'Take your thumb away, I can't hear you.' The nursery nurse removes his thumb and Ryan says 'Blocks'.

09.20   Ryan has built a ramp and walkway with the large wooden blocks. He has been assisted by another child. There has been no conversation but they appear to have agreed where things should go. Another child comes over and picks up one of the blocks from the walkway. Ryan looks up and runs over shouting 'No, no'. He pushes the child, who hastily drops the block. A member of staff tells Ryan not to push as it isn't kind. Ryan proceeds to pile up the blocks and sit on them. Anyone who comes near is scowled at. One of the other children has told a member of staff that Ryan won't let her play. The nursery nurse goes over and asks Ryan to share but he shakes his head. She tries to reason with him and when this doesn't work she moves him off the blocks. He races round the room bumping into several children.

09.35   The children are putting on coats to go outside. Ryan is persuaded to fasten his jacket and runs out to claim one of the bikes. He pedals well and is able to steer round corners. Another child is inside a tunnel which is being rocked by one of the staff. Ryan gets off the bike and joins him. They giggle together as the tunnel moves.

09.45   Ryan leaves the tunnel and walks towards a car. Another child also moves towards the car. Ryan starts to climb in but the other child pulls his coat from behind. Ryan turns and hits the boy, who starts to cry. Ryan is told to go and sit down until he can behave. He hunches up on the seat and starts to chew his coat sleeve.

09.55   The children go in to wash their hands for snack time. Ryan enjoys playing with the water. He goes through into the area where the tables are set with mugs. He chooses one seat but when a member of staff sits down beside him, he turns his head and moves to the next seat. A jug of milk is passed round and the children help themselves. Ryan manages to pour out some milk which he drinks very quickly. He takes a biscuit, and when reminded, manages to say thank you although he doesn't look directly at the speaker.

10.10   The children have been talking about what they have been doing this morning. Ryan remembers he played with the blocks and went on the bike but only uses single words.

10.15   Ryan and his group are sitting at the table. The nursery nurse has brought a bowl of water and some objects and is explaining that they are going to see if the things will sink or float. Each child takes a turn to put something into the water. The answers are often guesses but they all have a try including Ryan. At the end of the session the children can choose what to do next. Ryan chooses to stay with the water.

10.45   Ryan is making quite a mess so the nursery nurse puts a cloth on the floor and stands the bowl on it. He continues to drop objects into the water. The nursery nurse decides to make notes about Ryan's ability to predict floating or sinking. He ignores her at first but does eventually answer and manages to get some of the answers right. He finishes with the water and goes over to the trays of toys. He takes the train set, tips it out onto the floor and starts to make a line of track. Another child comes over and makes a separate line. They continue independently. Occasionally Ryan puts a piece of track into his mouth and sucks it.

11.00   The children are warned that they have 5 more minutes before it is time to clear up. The track reaches across the floor, and staff and children have been stepping over it. A nursery nurse accidentally kicks a piece and Ryan scowls. He starts to throw pieces around. When asked to stop and begin clearing up he runs under the table.

11.15   A member of staff is sitting next to the table trying to coax Ryan out. When asked if he wants to come and listen to the story he shakes his head. Eventually he is persuaded to come out and sit on the mat, but he shuffles backwards away from the group. He is taken aside and asked why he is so cross today. He has his thumb in his mouth and just looks blankly.

At 11.30 Ryan is collected by his dad, who asks 'Have you been good today?'

Evaluation
Ryan has good motor skills and can engage in imaginative play. His cognitive development is difficult to assess because of his language problems, but he did seem to have some understanding of floating and sinking.

Ryan plays alongside children but seldom interacts. He does not often make eye contact. He is still putting objects into his mouth.

Ryan is said to have 'a short fuse' and he reacts by throwing, pushing or hitting when upset. However, observation showed that he did not always start the trouble.

Ryan starts school in six months' time and will find it very difficult with the larger groups and fewer adults. He is seeing the speech therapist now and has an appointment for assessment by the educational psychologist. The family are known to social services, who have recently helped them to be rehoused, but they are still in high-rise accommodation.

Ryan has a lot of problems and may need to have learning support eventually, but in the meantime, what can you do to help?

1. Part of Ryan's problem may be that he has little opportunity to use up physical energy in the flat. He is rather boisterous so try to programme some physical activity before expecting him to sit and concentrate.

2. Discuss with your manager the possibility of a meeting with the speech therapist in order to plan activities which will encourage clearer speech, as part of the problem is Ryan's inability at times to make himself understood.

3. Encourage him to make more eye contact. This needs to be carefully managed so as not to appear threatening - maybe looking in mirrors first.

4. Try to distract him when he puts objects in his mouth by finding something interesting to do.

5. Encourage him to refrain from pushing and hitting by introducing a star chart for helpful behaviour, remembering that he is not always

the instigator of the problem. Children quickly recognize that some members of the group are 'always in trouble' and this can lead to them being blamed for everything.

6. As with all children, you should be trying to 'catch him being good', and praising to reinforce the behaviour.

You will need to continue to monitor Colin and Ryan to see if there is any improvement. You will also need to work with your nursery team, the parents and other professionals in order to provide continuity.

The last observation is of an 11-year-old in Year 6, who will be taking Key Stage 2 SATs at the end of the term. His practice results show that he is above average in numeracy but below in literacy. This is put down to the fact that he is a British Asian, but his spoken English is very good and many of the numeracy questions are in problem form, which he reads easily. He is in the middle group for reading, which shows that he is average in this area.

The observation is in time sampling format in order to cover concentration, rather than looking only at the results of writing.

Observation

Setting   A Year 6 classroom. Following the day's timetable displayed on the board the children come to sit on the mat for 'literacy hour'. The lesson today covers goals linked to 'modelled writing'.

10.05   M sits on the carpet and watches as the class teacher switches on the 'Word' presentation linked to Greek myths. There are several interruptions when children ask questions but M sits quietly. The teacher explains that the screen is the beginning of a story about Odysseus, and the children will be writing their own beginning for a myth. (This will contain Key Stage 2 targets.) M has moved back from the group but still appears to be concentrating on what is being said. The teacher asks questions but M does not put up his hand.

10.15   The group are asked to recall a previous story opening. M drops his head on to his knees for a few seconds but looks up when the teacher writes the learning objective - 'Can I write the opening of a myth?' The teacher starts the story off. She tells the group they can meet one of their objectives by finding really good objectives. She starts writing 'Looking down from his . . .' and asks for words to describe his palace. M puts up his hand and is chosen - he says 'snowy'. The teacher records his idea, then goes around the rest of the children with their hands up. M listens to the other children. The teacher writes a sentence - asking for ideas - and explains the use of a comma to make complex sentences.

10.25   M is still sat a little apart but he listens as the lesson proceeds. He stops looking ahead and smiles at another child, then he watches as two children start whispering to each other. The teacher calls the class to order. She explains, 'We've read the beginning of the story, I've modelled with new sentences, now it's your turn to write.' M returns to his desk with the rest of his group. He gets out his book then chats to friends on his table and takes some time to settle down.

10.30   M writes the date and learning objectives. He is unsure how to start the task as he missed yesterday's planning. I intervene and find out from the teacher what he needs. She gives M pictures of a hero, an enemy and a weapon. We discuss how these will fit into the story and check the target. M starts to write. His spelling is erratic but he has lots of ideas. Unfortunately, he goes off on a tangent - writing an adventure. I remind him that first he needs to describe the setting using adjectives. (Several other children also need to be reminded of this.)

10.40   M has crossed out his original work and written three lines about where Hermes lives. He is left handed and his letters tend to be of different sizes, making the work look rather messy. He has used capital letters and full stops, but there are several spelling mistakes. I go over this with him, and write some of the words in his spelling book. We talk about lessons and which ones he enjoys most. He likes mathematics and IT, which are the subjects he is in the top group for. He admits that he doesn't like writing.

10.50   The teacher asks the group to come back to the mat with their books. She invites children to read out their work. M does not volunteer. He sits quietly, but does not seem to be listening very closely. The teacher asks children to self-assess by putting their work to be marked in one of the boxes - green for 'I can do it', yellow for 'I think I've got it but would like some help', or red for 'I don't understand. I need more help'. M puts his book in the red box.

Evaluation

M does not have too much trouble concentrating. He is not part of the group who tend to have private chats. However, he sits back and his body language suggests that he doesn't really want to take an active part in discussions. When he did put his hand up the teacher chose him straight away as this was unusual. His spelling is poor and being left handed does not help the appearance of his work. However, his basic understanding does not seem to be linked to poorer performance in this subject. He has shown that he doesn't lack intelligence by his above average ability in mathematics.

M is lucky to be in a class that has only 18 children. The teacher is able to give him attention and praise when he makes a suggestion. It is difficult to make exceptions when all the children are getting ready to take the SATs test, but a possible short-term solution might be to allow M to compose his written work on the computer for part of the time. This could improve his spelling and the appearance of his work. He could concentrate on what he wants to say rather than the actual writing.

When M moves on to secondary school next year most subjects will require written projects. It would be a great advantage if he had gained more confidence before this happens.

Professionals you may meet as part of your role

Health Service

Family doctor (GP)

Everybody is entitled to be registered with a GP. Family doctors work in the community, sometimes alone but more usually as a member of a group practice. They are often based in a Health Centre with other professionals. Many centres have Well Person Clinics and Well Baby Clinics run in conjunction with the Health Visitor. Referrals are made to specialists and paramedical services if necessary.

Health Visitor

Health Visitors are qualified nurses who have undertaken further specialist training in midwifery, child development and preventive medicine. They work exclusively in the community and are usually attached to a GP practice. They work mainly with the under-5s but may continue to support families who have special need. They routinely screen children for hearing and vision defects, and carry out developmental checks.

Physiotherapist

The majority of physiotherapists work in hospitals, but some work in special schools or development assessment centres. They assess children's motor development and skills, and provide activities and exercises that parents and carers can use to encourage better mobility and co-ordination.

Occupational therapist

Occupational therapists work in hospitals, residential schools and development assessment centres. They will make home/school visits if necessary in order to advise about specialist equipment to encourage independent life skills. They assess children's practical abilities and advise on the most appropriate activities.

Speech therapist

Speech therapists may be employed in schools, in hospitals and in the community. They assess a child's speech, tongue and mouth movements and understanding of language. They provide exercises and activities both to develop all aspects of children's spoken and receptive communication skills and to encourage language development.

Clinical psychologist

Clinical psychologists are usually based in hospitals, but some work from Health Centres. They assess children's social and emotional development and are often involved when children are said to have 'behavioural' difficulties. They often work with social services in planning programmes at family centres.

Social services

Social worker

Most social workers now work in specialist teams such as those concerned with disability, the elderly and child protection. They support families and assess their needs. They are responsible for running family centres and for the registration of day nurseries and childminders. They are normally the prime workers when children are placed on 'at risk' registers or need court orders to protect them.

Family centre worker

Family centre workers are trained nursery nurses who work with social services at family centres (previously day nurseries). The centres provide support for carers and children who are experiencing problems, perhaps caused by disability or a perceived lack of parenting skills.

Education

Educational psychologist

Educational psychologists are involved in the educational assessment of children with special needs. They use a battery of tests to try to establish these needs in order to prepare a statement of Special Educational Needs.

They act as advisors to professionals working directly with children who have a range of conditions which affect their ability to learn.

Special Educational Needs Co-ordinator (SENCO)

SENCOs advise teachers and support staff working with children who have been identified as having a special educational need. They also liaise with colleagues in special schools and with parents. They are responsible for co-ordinating provision for children including the IEP (individual education plan), for keeping the school's Special Educational Needs (SEN) register and for working with external agencies.

Special needs teacher

Special needs teachers are qualified teachers with additional training and experience in working with children who have learning difficulties. They may work in a special school or be based in a unit in a mainstream school. There are also peripatetic teachers who visit children in mainstream schools. They may specialize in a particular disorder such as vision or hearing impairment.

Special needs support assistant

Special needs support assistants work in both special and mainstream schools. They often work with individual statemented children, but are also involved with groups of children who are under-achieving. They usually work in the classroom under the direction of the teacher, but they also meet regularly with the SENCO to discuss planning. They may be qualified nursery nurses or undertake in-service training such as the Certificate in Learning Support.

REFERENCES

Berryman, J., Hargreaves, D.J., Howells, K. and Ockleford, E. (2002) *Developmental Psychology & You* (2nd edn). Oxford: Blackwell.

Fishbein, H. (1984) *The Psychology of Infancy and Childhood: Evolutionary and Cross Cultural Perspectives.* Hillsdale NJ: Erlbaum.

Grieve, R. and Hughes, M (eds) (1990) *Understanding Children.* Oxford: Blackwell.

Ott, P. (1997) *How to Detect and Manage Dyslexia.* London: Heinemann.

Tough, J. (1976) *Listening to Children Talking.* London: Ward Lock Education.

CHAPTER FIVE

Linking Observations and Assessments to the Curriculum

At the end of this chapter you will:

- **Have an awareness of the six areas of learning and the early learning goals.**

- **Have an awareness of the Foundation Stage Profile.**

- **Understand more fully the partnership between parents and carers.**

In September 2002 *Early Learning Goals for the Foundation Stage* replaced *Nursery Education: Desirable Outcomes for Children's Learning on Entering Compulsory Education*.

The period from age three to the end of the reception year is described as the foundation stage. It is a distinct stage and important both in its own right and in preparing children for later schooling. The early learning goals set out what is expected for most children by the end of the foundation stage.

The foundation stage begins when children reach the age of three. Many children first attend some form of pre-school or nursery soon after their third birthday. Children may go to a number of settings during the foundation stage; they may attend part time or full time; a few will stay at home until they begin primary school.

> The last year of the foundation stage is often described as the reception year, since most children are admitted to the reception class of a primary school at some point during the year.
>
> (*Early Learning Goals*, DfEE/QCA)

Areas of Learning and Early Learning Goals

The foundation stage of the curriculum is organized into six areas of learning:

- personal, social and emotional development;
- communication, language and literacy;
- mathematical development;

- knowledge and understanding of the world;
- physical development;
- creative development.

The early learning goals establish expectations for most children to reach by the end of the foundation stage. They are organized into the six areas of the curriculum and provide the basis for planning throughout the foundation stage, so laying secure foundations for future learning. By the end of the foundation stage, some children will have exceeded the goals. Other children will still be working towards some or all of the goals.

Below are the early learning goals for each area of learning, taken from *Early Learning Goals* (DfEE/QCA).

Early Learning Goals for Personal, Social and Emotional Development

By the end of the foundation stage, most children will:

- continue to be interested, excited and motivated to learn;
- be confident to try new activities, initiate ideas and speak in a familiar group;
- maintain attention, concentrate and sit quietly when appropriate;
- have a developing awareness of their own needs, views and feelings and be sensitive to the needs, views and feelings of others;
- have a developing respect for their own cultures and beliefs and those of other people;
- respond to significant experiences, showing a range of feelings when appropriate;
- form good relationships with adults and peers;
- work as part of a group or class, taking turns and sharing fairly, understanding that there needs to be agreed values and codes of behaviour for groups of people, including adults and children, to work together harmoniously;
- understand what is right, what is wrong, and why;
- dress and undress independently and manage their own personal hygiene;
- select and use activities and resources independently;
- consider the consequences of their words and actions for themselves and others;
- understand that people have different needs, views, cultures and beliefs, which need to be treated with respect;
- understand that they can expect others to treat their needs, views, cultures and beliefs with respect.

Early Learning Goals for Communication, Language and Literacy

By the end of the foundation stage, most children will be able to:

- enjoy listening to and using spoken and written language, and readily turn to it in their play and learning;
- explore and experiment with sounds, words and texts;
- listen with enjoyment and respond to stories, songs and other music, rhymes and poems, and make up their own stories, songs, rhymes and poems;

Figure 5.1 Role play: 'Hello – who's there?'

- use language to imagine and recreate roles and experiences;
- use talk to organize, sequence and clarify thinking, ideas, feelings and events;
- sustain attentive listening, responding to what they have heard by relevant comments, questions or actions;
- interact with others, negotiating plans and activities and taking turns in conversation;
- extend their vocabulary, exploring the meanings and sounds of new words;
- retell narratives in the correct sequence, drawing on the language patterns of stories;
- speak clearly and audibly with confidence and control and show awareness of the listener, for example by their use of conventions such as greetings, 'please' and 'thank you';
- hear and say initial and final sounds in words, and short vowel sounds within words;
- link sounds to letters, naming and sounding the letters of the alphabet;
- read independently a range of familiar and common words and simple sentences;
- know that print carries meaning and, in English, is read from left to right and top to bottom;
- show an understanding of the elements of stories, such as main character, sequence of events and openings, and of how information can be found in non-fiction texts to answer questions about where, who, why and how;
- attempt writing for various purposes, using features of different forms such as lists, stories and instructions;
- write their own names and other things such as labels and captions and begin to form simple sentences, sometimes using punctuation;
- use their phonic knowledge to write simple regular words and make phonetically plausible attempts at more complex words;
- use a pencil and hold it effectively to form recognizable letters, most of which are correctly formed.

Early Learning Goals for Mathematical Development

By the end of the foundation stage, most children will be able to:

- say and use number names in order in familiar contexts;
- count reliably up to 10 everyday objects;
- recognize numerals 1 to 9;
- use language such as 'more' or 'less', 'greater' or 'smaller', 'heavier' or 'lighter', to compare two numbers or quantities;
- in practical activities and discussion, begin to use the vocabulary involved in adding and subtracting;
- find one more or one less than a number from 1 to 10;
- begin to relate addition to combining two groups of objects, and subtraction to 'taking away';
- talk about, recognize and recreate simple patterns;
- use language such as 'circle' or 'bigger' to describe the shape and size of solids and flat shapes;
- use everyday words to describe position;
- use developing mathematical ideas and methods to solve practical problems.

Early Learning Goals for Knowledge and Understanding of the World

By the end of the foundation stage, most children will be able to:

- investigate objects and materials by using all of their senses as appropriate;
- find out about, and identify some features of, living things, objects and events they observe;
- look closely at similarities, differences, patterns and change;
- ask questions about why things happen and how things work;
- build and construct with a wide range of objects, selecting appropriate resources and adapting their work where necessary;
- select the tools and techniques they need to shape, assemble and join the materials they are using;
- find out about, and identify the uses of, everyday technology and use information and communication technology and programmable toys to support their learning;
- find out about past and present events in their own lives, and in those of their families and other people they know;
- observe, find out about, and identify features in the place where they live and the natural world;
- begin to know about their own cultures and beliefs and those of other people;
- find out about their environment, and talk about those features they like and dislike.

Early Learning Goals for Physical Development

By the end of the foundation stage, most children will be able to:

- move with confidence, imagination and in safety;
- move with control and co-ordination;
- show awareness of space, of themselves and of others;

Figure 5.2 Learning together: enjoying each other's company

- recognize the importance of keeping healthy and those things which contribute to this;
- recognize the changes that happen to their bodies when they are active;
- use a range of small and large equipment;
- travel around, under, over and through balancing and climbing equipment;
- handle tools, objects, construction and malleable materials safely and with increasing control.

Early Learning Goals for Creative Development

By the end of the foundation stage, most children will be able to:

- explore colour, texture, shape, form and space in two and three dimensions;
- recognize and explore how sounds can be changed, sing simple songs from memory, recognize repeated sounds and sound patterns and match movements to music;
- respond in a variety of ways to what they see, hear, smell, touch and feel;
- use their imagination in art and design, music, dance, imaginative and role play and stories;
- express and communicate their ideas, thoughts and feelings by using a widening range of materials, suitable tools, imaginative and role play, movement, designing and making, and a variety of songs and musical instruments.

The Foundation Stage Profile

The Foundation Stage Profile is the statutory assessment for children in their final year of the foundation stage. This profile replaced the baseline assessment in September 2002 and the first children's profiles were completed at the end of the summer term in 2003. Baseline assessments had been used in schools in England and Wales since September 1998 and employed the desirable outcomes as criteria for the assessment. The Qualifications and Curriculum Authority (QCA) chose the word 'profile' carefully because it reflects a new approach to assessment. The Foundation Stage Profile reflects what a child has achieved, knows and can do. It is based on the early learning goals and on *Curriculum Guidance for the Foundation Stage*. There is no testing, there are no tasks, but rather a profile compiled by Early Years practitioners. The profile also includes other contributions from those involved with the assessment process: observations by nursery nurses, learning assistants and other practitioners, the child's parents or carers, the child and any records from previous settings. The Foundation Stage Profile is about assessment for learning – observations.

Throughout a child's foundation stage, Early Years practitioners will need to assess the child's development in relation to the stepping-stones and early learning goals that form part of *Curriculum Guidance for the Foundation Stage*. Assessments should be based on the practitioner's accumulating observations and their knowledge of the whole child. At the end of the last year in the foundation stage, the Foundation Stage Profile will provide a summary of the knowledge of the child.

A practitioner will complete a Foundation Stage Profile using a set of 13 assessment scales, each of which has 9 points. Early learning goals are presented individually or have been split or combined as appropriate, to assist completion. At the end of the reception class the teacher or practitioner will record each item that the child has achieved on each scale, and each point will have been considered separately. For each scale point a judgement will be made by the practitioner and will represent their assessment of the child's typical attainment. In many cases, practitioners will be able to make judgements in relation to the scale from their knowledge of the child and the ongoing development in the learning and teaching. At times further information to support the practitioner's judgements may be necessary and additional observations have to be undertaken.

Regular observations and assessment will enhance children's learning and development. Skilled observations of children can be utilized by practitioners, who should carefully analyse and evaluate the observation, recording the essential information regarding the child's progress and development. These observations of an individual child's development can then be used to help provide an appropriate curriculum for each child. Observations of each child should be undertaken regularly. The contexts should be part of the normal curriculum provision, within which the assessment observations are planned and integrated.

Good observations enable a setting to:

- Assess what a child has learned in relation to the six areas of learning and record this on assessment scales for the Foundation Stage Profile.
- Assess and record the stage of development the child has reached.
- Plan a balanced curriculum, based on the needs of the child, and continuity and progression for each child. These next stages must be based on a knowledge and understanding of individual children's experience and understanding.
- Identify any special educational needs and formulate an individual educational plan if necessary.

Key Stages 1–4 of the National Curriculum of England and Wales follow on from the foundation stage and will cover the child from the age of 6 years up to 16. At the end of each stage there are tests – Statutory Attainment Tests (SATs). Up until Key Stage 3 (Years 1–9) all children in state schools follow a curriculum of compulsory subjects. At age 14 children are required to take further tests to enable teachers and pupils to decide which optional subjects they will study for their GCSE. Each Key Stage is divided into levels and this gives an indication of whether the child is operating at the correct stage or is above or below. We do not intend to list subjects here, but if you are interested in learning more about Key Stages and testing you can log on to www.direct.gov.uk, then follow Education and learning, Schools, Understanding the curriculum. (Readers in Scotland can log on to http://www.scotland.gov.uk/Topics/Education/Schools/curriculum for information on the Scottish school system, and those in the Republic of Ireland can look at http://www.ncca.ie/)

Formal observations are not as common after the foundation stage as most of the testing is linked to specific tasks, e.g within a reading assessment during Year 6 the teacher listens to the child read aloud and notes pronunciation, stopping at punctuation marks, expression, etc. However, linking observations to Key Stages can sometimes give a clearer picture of children's individual needs.

SATs practice tests give an indication of areas that need to be revised, but they show only if the answer is right or wrong. Even if the child shows working it is not always possible to see how they were thinking. Observing how children are working, which questions are taking time, and asking questions afterwards about why they did something a certain way can give a much better indication of individual need.

Here is an example of a question from a practice paper for levels 3–5 in Key Stage 2.

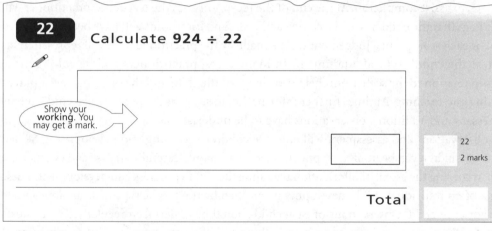

Figure 5.3

The way that children tackled this varied.

Several children drew 22 circles and attempted to put dashes in each to count up to 924.

One child did the following calculations:

$$4 \div 22$$
$$20 \div 22$$
$$900 \div 22$$

One child attempted to complete a 22 times table.

One child tried an inverse multiplication. He had worked out that 50 times would be too large, so he did trial and error starting at 22×45 to end up at the right answer of 42.

Looking at the observations, the teacher had a better idea of the problem and was able to revise division by 'chunking'.

Partnership with Parents: Ways of Sharing Information

Parents are a valuable resource when assessing a child's development. They know a great deal about their own children. They have background information that will have a definite impact on how the child works through a variety of experiences and environments. As children often behave in a manner that has a direct link to the home environment, it makes sense to use this valuable resource.

Many factors will influence how we do this in order to achieve what is best for the families and their individual children. There will always be a variety of styles and levels of parenting, and a great variation in the levels of interest shown in children's education. Parents are concerned about the quality of care and education their children are receiving, but some feel that it is totally the teacher's role to 'educate'. These tend to be confident in the care being given and the level of learning achieved. A positive inspection report is all they need to affirm their faith in the school. They only become involved if there is a problem. Other parents like to follow their child's progress carefully and to be involved in every aspect of their developments and learning. They visit often, volunteer for a variety of tasks and attend meetings.

There are also parents who would like to be more involved, but are overwhelmed or alienated by institutions and schools. Staff may mistakenly interpret their non-attendance at school functions and meetings as being due to a lack of interest. It is also essential to schedule meetings when parents (particularly working parents) can attend. The provision of crèche facilities for younger siblings should be included in meeting announcements. The goal is to establish and maintain partnerships with all parents.

We should all have the same aim: **to help the child develop and extend their learning**. One of the key principles of the foundation stage, as stated by the Qualifications and Curriculum Authority (QCA), is that 'parents and practitioners should work together in an atmosphere of mutual respect within which children can have security and confidence'. To achieve this we need to share experiences and information about the child. How can this be accomplished? Here are some suggestions:

- Take every opportunity to chat informally with parents.
- Talk about and record information about the child's progress and achievements – make a book about the child with the child contributing.
- Keep a brief record so that you know which parents you haven't talked to recently, and which parents are taking up most of your time.
- Share information passed on by parents with other members of staff. Some of this information may be very important to the child's welfare but may not be formally recorded, e.g. a father's absence or a grandmother's illness.
- Parents can report through a 'home setting diary' on activities and visits undertaken.
- Send home small assignments, e.g. 'Find out about . . .'
- Plan an area where children, parents and staff can display photographic evidence of a variety of events and activities. These can be used for the group or individual photo albums – a yearbook to which everyone involved with the child can contribute. Special events can be videoed and the video loaned to parents. This requires careful organization but an interested parent might be willing to do this. Older children might take it on as a project in the design and technology curriculum. Regular 'feature films' on school life could be just the thing to attract parents into the classroom.

Pastoral care is a very important area to consider. Parents are happy when things are going well. We need to help them to support children when things are not as satisfactory. Educational progress is important, but when parents feel pressurized by other parents, teachers or the media about their child's ability to read, for example, it puts extra strain on the family and this is not helpful to the child. It is essential that parents know the expectations of the nursery and school, how they can support and encourage their children and who to go to for help if there is a problem.

We also need to ask ourselves if families feel comfortable with all aspects of the school environment. Have their family structures been accommodated by the establishment – their cultures, languages and religious beliefs? Do we check with parents what they really want or do we decide first what we expect and then assume that parents will follow our guidelines? If parents do not conform and do not seem interested, have we asked them the reason for this? Does the school programme positively reflect the cultural, language and faith diversity of the families? Are the school guidelines discussed and negotiated with parents? Do school staff make planned and energetic attempts to involve all parents, rather than automatically assuming lack of interest?

Here are a few of the many innovative ways that have been devised to make partnerships possible with all parents:

- Provide a family room where parents can meet, relax and share experiences and where teachers can drop in for an informal chat.
- Keep parents fully informed about the curriculum through brochures, displays and videos.
- Plan a workshop on the way reading is taught in the school. This can inform parents about useful ways to help their children at home.
- Encourage parents to stay and watch the children working on occasion, so that they can understand the aims and objectives of the teaching. Provide an outline of the term's activities and how parents and other family members might help.
- Invite parents to contribute ideas and objects for displays linked to the area of learning. Families who have lived locally for several years will enjoy the opportunity to contribute to a school project, and it may foster a greater sense of belonging among newcomers.
- Involve parents in decisions about the topics and timing of open days, parents' evenings and workshops in order to enable as many as possible to attend.
- Encourage parents to borrow books to share with their children at home.

CHAPTER SIX

Activities to Assist Curriculum Planning in order to Promote Developmental Progress

The main reason why we observe children is to see what they are able to do in order to plan how to lead them forward. In Chapter 3 examples of observations were given together with evaluations that suggested activities which would help children overcome a difficulty or perfect a skill. For example, if a child has difficulty cutting out with scissors, then we would provide exercises to strengthen finger muscles and increase opportunities for practice. If children lack concentration, we would develop games and activities to help their listening skills and maintain their interest. If they have problems integrating with other children, we would think about ways to encourage them first to work with another child and adult, then in a small group. In each case the activities we provide would come about as a result of carefully observing the children in order to assess their needs.

The activities that follow have been arranged in age progression but the headings are only guidelines. They do relate to developmental progress so they can be adapted for individual children whose needs have been identified, and who may be functioning at an earlier or later stage. They have been grouped into areas of development that relate to early learning goals for the foundation stage to enable you to think about progression in your planning, but they can be used with Key Stage 1 children, especially in after-school clubs. The activities also cover babies and toddlers. They are arranged under the same headings but essentially relate to the 'Strong Child', 'Skilful Communicator' and 'Competent Learner' sections of *Birth to Three Matters* – the initiative to develop a framework to support practitioners working with children under 3. The sections covering ages 9–16 years have been arranged more informally. They briefly discuss development at various stages and make suggestions for the types of activities enjoyed. They concentrate on out-of-school activities when children choose what they want to do: the time when the adult becomes the facilitator for children and young people, rather than the organizer all the time.

The lists are certainly not definitive. They are meant to trigger your own thoughts about providing valuable experiences for the children in your care.

Curriculum Area – Physical development

Physical development is about improving children's skills of co-ordination, control over their bodies, manipulation and movement.

We should consider planning activities that will provide the correct level of challenge. We need to provide resources that can be used in a variety of ways and a variety of situations. Planning should also consider the language used to describe movements, the needs of children with a physical disability and how to supervise children safely without undermining their independence.

Gross Motor Skills

Age group 0–1 year

Non-mobile babies need you to be the instigator of movement – take their hands in order to play Pat-a-cake, move their legs in a *cycling motion* especially at nappy change, encourage babies to feel their feet and *bounce up and down* while in the adult grasp.

Allow time on the floor to *push up onto arms* to get ready to *crawl*. (For babies who have poor muscle control a wedge-shaped piece of foam will provide support under the chest.)

Give baby an opportunity to *crawl* safely by providing space – rolling toys will encourage them to move.

Provide sturdy furniture, allowing the child to *pull to stand*. Encourage the year-old child to *walk round* the playpen and provide opportunities for safe supported walking, e.g. push-along toys such as a trolley with bricks.

Age group 1–4 years

Continue to provide toys that will assist *walking*.

Encourage toddlers' mobility by providing balls to *run* after. Young children love to *throw* things and this can be channelled into games using balls.

Introduce language to use movement to express feelings, adjust speed or change direction to avoid obstacles and experiment with different ways of moving.

Sing songs like 'Head, shoulders, knees and toes' to help children's awareness of their bodies.

Play games like Ring O'Roses.

Provide access to large mobile toys like tricycles, wheelbarrows and doll's prams.

Provide access to safe climbing toys at the nursery or the park.

Music and movement – make a tape of music that changes rhythm, speed and volume. Ask the children to listen and then move to the music – encourage a lot of experimenting by introducing words like slither, shuffle, crawl, jump, skip, gallop, high, low, etc. (For younger children or those with English as a second language, remember that there is an increased need to demonstrate.) In order to extend children's knowledge of other cultures you can use different musical instruments.

Dodgem cars – ask the children to walk slowly round the room moving in and out of each other but not bumping. Increase the pace to jogging and then running if there is sufficient space. Slow down gradually. If the children are managing to avoid bumping you could extend the skills by asking the children to walk backwards.

A catch circle game – form a small group of children into a circle, then stand in the middle and throw a variety of large balls and bean bags to the children to encourage catching and throwing skills. For younger children and those with motor impairments the ball needs to be quite large and thrown into the child's arms.

Age group 4–8 years

The same activities as for younger children but with increased skill.

This is a very active period in children's lives. They will normally exercise freely without much help from adults.

Provide safe, supervised areas for children to run, climb, balance, dance. Encourage children to refine their skills during organized games and PE sessions.

Be aware that some children will have difficulty with balance and co-ordination, so provide activities where they can be successful.

Follow my Leader – set out some hoops or coiled rope for the children to avoid. Ask the children to follow you with the music and move around the room leaping, jumping, turning and hopping. Use large, exaggerated movements. Then allow the child behind you to take the lead.

Outdoor/indoor activity circuit – lay out hoops, skipping ropes, balancing bars, tunnels and slides and supervise the children as they go round the circuit. Younger children will need more adult supervision; older children may turn the game into a timed activity in order to practise improving their skills.

A catch circle – as with the younger children but using smaller balls, beanbags and frisbees. This can be done in the circle or with children working in pairs.

Team games involving bats like rounders and cricket can be introduced as the children reach seven, but such games take a lot of practice and not all children will be very successful.

Fine Motor Skills

Age group 0–1 year

Mobiles and *pram beads* should be placed near the baby to encourage reaching out to feel.

Encourage the 6- to 12-month baby to play with nesting cubes and beakers, floating bath toys, plastic saucepans and lids. Use shakers which can easily be held, cotton reels and activity centres with different actions that the baby can move. Just remember that all young children explore with their mouth, so make sure the equipment is washable.

All babies love toys that are brightly coloured and make a noise, but these are particularly important if they have a sight problem.

Age group 1–4 years

During these years children are gaining much more control of fine movements and usually develop a hand preference.

Manipulative materials like Play-doh, modelling clay and bread dough will all help to strengthen fingers.

Figure 6.1 At 2: fine motor control now developing well

Finger painting, hand printing, splatter painting, sponge printing and cutting and sticking all help children to gain control. Children who have difficulty with cutting can be helped by using spring-handled scissors – and don't forget your left-handed children.

Construction toys such as Lego, wooden blocks, stickle bricks.

Table-top toys like jigsaws, mosaics, large bead threading.

Action nursery rhymes like 'Tommy Thumb'.

Figure 6.2 Providing a doll to dress helps refine motor skills

Age group 4–8 years

Junk modelling.

Crayon resist patterns.

Cutting and glueing – collage.

Puppet making.

Drawing, clay modelling, stencilling, paper folding, paper weaving, sewing.

More complex construction kits such as Meccano.

More complicated jigsaws and mosaics.

All these activities will help children's fine manipulative skills and eye–hand co-ordination, but at this age the end product will also be important.

When planning, do try to allow enough time to complete an activity, although by 6 or 7 years children should be able to leave and come back to a project.

Curriculum Area – Communication, Language and Literacy

Communication, language and literacy is about improving children's ability to communicate through verbal and non-verbal means, developing the ability to decipher symbols in order to read and experiencing writing for a range of purposes.

When planning activities we should always consider the opportunities for extending children's ability to listen to, speak, and see language. The ability to acquire language is at the heart of children's learning.

Age group 0–1 year

Talk and listen to the baby so that they learn speech is a two-way process.

Encourage listening skills by providing musical toys.

Introduce repetitive rhymes and songs – reinforced by actions.

Towards the end of the first year introduce simple picture books with one illustration to the page of familiar objects like cup, ball, teddy. You can also make your own book using photographs of family and objects from around the home.

Name parts of the body as you dress and undress the baby.

Age group 1–4 years

Continue talking and listening about everyday activities.

When saying nursery rhymes, stop before the last word to give the toddler a chance to complete it.

Sing naming rhymes, e.g. 'Tommy Thumb', 'This is the way we nod our head, brush our teeth', etc.

Introduce action songs like 'The wheels on the bus go round and round'.

Encourage listening skills with tapes and story books – especially those with repetition, like *The Enormous Turnip* and *The Very Hungry Caterpillar*, or any favourite stories, including those made up to include the child's name. (N.B. The names of the participants pulling up the turnip and the foods that the caterpillar eats can be adapted to names within the child's experience.)

Provide dressing-up clothes for role-play language.

Age group 4–8 years

Talk and listen to the children, using open-ended questions.

Introduce songs that the children can join in or make up for themselves.

Create opportunities for imaginative play, e.g. puppet theatres, home corners set up as shops, cafes, hospitals, hairdressers, etc.

Encourage an interest in books that gradually have more complicated plots and characters.

Encourage listening skills with games like Simon Says and Musical Statues, or identifying noises in a bingo quiz where the children listen to a tape of animal or household noises.

Play games like I Spy which make the children think about the sounds that letters make.

Label objects so that the child will recognize that written symbols stand for words.

Encourage children to write their own stories and letters – these can be recorded on tape if writing skills are not well developed.

Introduce children to poetry and rhymes. Have them write their own.

Make children think about language by making up riddles, e.g.

This is a word that rhymes with up.

You can drink out of me because I'm a (cup).

I'm brown and I'm hard, I grow in the ground.

When you've cooked me and peeled me, I'm soft, white and round (potato).

Have a 'Round the World Week' where the children learn how to write the words for hello and goodbye in as many languages as possible in order to understand the concept of symbols standing for meaning. This can also be extended into sign language and picture language, e.g. the willow pattern plate telling a story, or tracking signs.

Curriculum Area – Creative Development

Children's creativity develops best in a rich learning environment, supported by adults providing the opportunity to experiment with new materials and ideas. We need to be sensitive to children's pace of learning and make sure our activities do not rely on a 'perfect' end product. This area of learning should include activities linked to art, music, dance, role play and imaginative play. It should involve children responding by using all their senses.

Age group 0–2 years

Babies explore their environment using their senses (sensory-motor period). Initially it will be up to the adult to provide the stimulus by singing, dancing holding the baby, hanging mobiles and pictures near to the crib, stroking when being bathed or changed. As babies learn to sit up and hold things, rattles and activity centres with different textures and sounds will allow the children to experiment for themselves. Musical instruments can be made using pots and wooden spoons from the kitchen. By the age of two you can have quite a band.

When providing different materials for babies to feel, remember that it is still natural for them to put everything into the mouth. So let them finger-feed (different taste sensations) and make the messy play using jelly or custard as opposed to thickened paint.

During their second year babies are gaining more control over their bodies. They also want to be more independent. Once walking, they like to dance to music and begin to imitate housework like sweeping and dusting. They are beginning to pretend to drink from plastic cups and feed the dolly. Simple role-play areas that reflect home are useful now.

Babies have little concept of 'art' but around 12–15 months they will have learned how to make marks on paper using a chunky crayon. They enjoy the 'doing' rather than any end result. Handprints with the adult painting a child's hand and pressing it onto the paper may make a nice souvenir, but does not really have much value as a learning experience. Try putting the paint onto the table and allowing the toddler to spread it around – then take a print of the pattern they have made.

By the age of two, children can experiment with pencils, crayons, chalks and paint. Small groups, closely supervised, should be able to decide how they want to use the materials.

Age group 2–4 years

Children are beginning to have a better sense of rhythm and will enjoy dancing to a tape, singing or using instruments. Encourage children to think about how they are moving – fast, slow, high, low.

When using musical instruments, encourage the children to listen to the sounds and to think about the way the noise is produced – do we shake, bang, blow? Try to introduce instruments from other countries and different types of music – classical, reggae and pop as well as the more familiar nursery rhymes.

Encourage children to listen to everyday sounds – try a sound walk which older children can record when they get back (see Figure 6.3).

Children in this age group will continue to imitate but are also beginning to use their imagination. Role play can be extended by providing boxes and lengths of cloth which can be turned into anything.

Figure 6.3

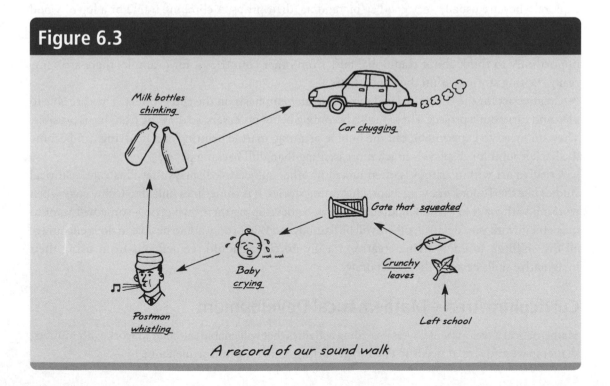

Milk bottles chinking

Car chugging

Gate that squeaked

Baby crying

Crunchy leaves

Postman whistling

Left school

A record of our sound walk

The home corner is still valuable as an intimate area where children can relax and act out their stories, but can also be extended to cover 'knowledge of the world' by changing to a supermarket, post office or doctor's surgery.

In creative art the process is still as important as the end product but children will begin to think about planning what they want to do. Provide a wide variety of materials for junk modelling so that they can choose. Let them experiment with lots of different media: thick and thin paint, crayons, chalks, charcoal. Encourage mixing colours and making colours light and dark. Use different stimuli as a trigger for creative activities – music, stories, puppets. This will enable children to choose how they want to work. If you want to link a display to a certain topic then you can make the story reflect that topic without dictating exactly how it will be set out. Younger children can look at pictures from a story in order to choose, but as they get older they should be able to tell you which parts they have enjoyed most and would like to display.

You can also begin to think about other craft forms like pottery, weaving, sewing and various forms of printing on material.

Age group 4–8 years

At this stage music and movement should progress from making sounds and following rhythm to being able to follow a tune. By the age of eight children are often able to 'compose' their own tunes on the xylophone.

Music can be combined with drama and children will be able to learn lines and repeat dance movements. However, there should also be plenty of time for experimenting with new sounds and movements. As with the younger group, you can enrich children's experiences by providing instruments and taped music from a variety of cultures.

Children will still enjoy domestic role play but as they get older their play often becomes more influenced by the television they watch and the books they read. What they need most is space to explore. They are usually very good at 'pretending' their props. A climbing frame or a log of wood can become almost anything. Within the classroom children can make masks and costumes in order to engage in dramatic play – this can be extended to a class production of a story. This is another opportunity to think about traditional tales from other countries – for example, there are some really exciting stories within the Hindu faith.

Creative art for the 4-year-old will mean a greater emphasis on the end product. They are able to plan and carry out a project. They are also becoming better observers, so drawing from life is possible. They still need to experiment, but the bubble printing, marble printing and tie dying can become the background for displays – much more exciting than dull backing paper.

Creative art within school is often linked to other subjects – displays that illustrate historical studies like the Tudors, drawing maps, illustrating stories. It is sometimes linked to technology when working with ways to print. Children may now be developing their own style – some will want to make their work very detailed, others will be flamboyant. What you want to be able to do is encourage all the children to enjoy being creative. Ideally no child should feel left out from using their imaginative skills because they 'can't draw'.

Curriculum Area – Mathematical Development

Mathematical development covers providing activities that will enable the child to work with number, shape, space and size. It needs to encourage sorting, matching and sequencing.

Age group 0–2 years

Piaget called this age the 'sensory-motor' stage. This means that young children learn by exploring and touching, hearing things named and seeing number in a concrete way.

Talk about everyday objects like the *round* ball and the *red* bus.

Sing number rhymes:

'Ten little toes – one little nose';

'1, 2, 3, 4, 5 – once I caught a fish alive',

remembering to point as you count.

Count the stairs as you climb up.

Provide toys that are brightly coloured and have different textures and shape, which can be explored first with the mouth and then with fingers.

Building blocks are ideal for counting and talking about *building up* and *knocking down*.

Shape sorters allow the child to practise finding the right space – first by trial and error and then by recognition.

Stacking cups will begin to teach about space and size. (This can just as easily be old boxes of different sizes.)

Age group 2–4 years

Provide lots of opportunities for children to count – 'How many children are having lunch today?' 'How many cups must I put out?'

Include numbers on your displays so that children begin to see the connection between the number and the symbol that represents it.

Use sorting exercises like putting socks and shoes into pairs and clearing up toys into their right boxes.

If the child has a zoo or farmyard, put all the animals of one sort together. (This can lead to talk of big and small if the animals have young.)

Play simple matching games like picture dominoes. You can also make your own with cut-out shapes to match up. (For children who find this difficult you can give an extra clue – make the matching shapes the same colour.)

You can make big two- and three-dimensional shapes for the children to play with – talk about how many sides they have, if they roll, if they are flat.

Introduce action songs with counting:

'Five little ducks went swimming one day';

'Five currant buns (chapatis) in the baker's shop';

'Five speckled frogs'.

These are useful because they allow the child to start learning about subtraction.

Help concepts of volume by providing water play with jugs and beakers of various sizes.

Age group 4–8 years

Help concepts of volume by providing water play with calibrated jugs and beakers.

Help concepts of mass by providing sand and Play-doh which can be 'shared out'.

Help concepts of time by setting up friezes that show things we do when we get up, eat our breakfast, go to school, etc.

Sequencing activities – e.g. size:

Grow beans or sunflowers and plot their growth. (See Figure 6.4.)

Talk about and display frogspawn – tadpole – baby frog – adult frog.

Have a display showing baby – toddler – child – adult.

(Sequencing also helps left to right orientation – a prerequisite for reading.)

Sorting into different property sets, e.g. things that float or sink, those that are attracted by a magnet and those that are not.

Introduce games with a scoring system that require the child first to add on, then take away and finally multiply.

Curriculum Area – Personal, Social and Emotional Development

Creating an environment where children are able to feel positive about themselves, want to explore and experiment, and are able to work with others and independently is at the centre of good childcare practice. The activities you provide if you have carried out observations should be challenging, but not so far beyond the child's capabilities that they do not have the chance to succeed and feel good about themselves. Your observations should also alert you to children who have problems concentrating, which can lead to challenging behaviour.

Age group 0–1 year

Activities that will help the baby feel positive about themselves – smiling, playing Peek-a-boo, cuddling, answering back when they attempt to communicate.

Provide a mirror for babies to see how they look.

After 6 months allow the baby to finger-feed in safety.

At 9 months allow the baby to hold a spoon at mealtimes – although do not expect success at this age.

Age group 1–4 years

Continue to allow to finger-feed and hold a spoon, which should become more successful by 18 months.

Promote dressing skills by making a doll, book, etc. that will give practice at doing up buttons, buckles, zips and any other fastenings familiar to the child's mode of dress.

Provide clothing and utensils in the home corner which will reflect the child's home life and show that it is valued.

Age group 4–8 years

Allow sufficient time before and after a physical training session for the children to undress and dress by themselves.

Have a dressing-up race where children put on hats, gloves, etc.

Preparing and sharing a meal – this can be sandwiches at 4 years and gradually become more elaborate. (Try out recipes from around the world.)

Team building and working together can be improved by providing challenges which require co-operation. This can be to build a railway at 4 or a lighthouse with working parts at 8.

Display all of the children's work at some time so that they can share in the praise.

Activity

Parachute games suitable for 8 years plus

Swamp chute
One person plays the alligator and goes under the parachute.
Everyone else sits down with legs under the parachute.
Billow the parachute slightly but no one may look to see where the alligator is.
The alligator grabs someone's legs and pulls them under the parachute.
They become an alligator as well and pull others under until everyone becomes an alligator.

Tortoise
The parachute becomes a giant tortoise shell with everyone underneath on their hands and knees.
The idea is to make the tortoise move about, but remain in one piece.
Once it starts to move well, the tortoise can tackle an obstacle course, appropriate to the ability of the group involved.

Curriculum Area – Knowledge and Understanding of the World

The activities in this area of development are very closely linked to all the others. The main focus is on providing activities that will enable children to learn about their environment – which they will have been doing when they experiment with the properties of different materials in creative work. Babies will be learning about their world when they find out the words for objects. As the children get older they can learn about the wider environment – by going out into the community, having visits from different people, and eventually by using books, videos, maps, artefacts and other reference materials.

Age group 0–2 years

Encourage curiosity by providing materials that can be used in several ways – bricks, household articles like pots and pans and wooden spoons.

Name objects – talk about what they do.

Use books to show pictures of familiar objects, show the real object and name it, e.g. 'Look at the ball, here's a ball, what can we do with the ball?' In this way the child will learn that pictures can represent real things.

Involve the child in what you are doing if it is safe to do so. You may need to put them into a high chair if you are making cakes in the kitchen, but they can have a plastic bowl and spoon to stir.

As you walk along the road explain what you are seeing – the red bus, the cat, the milkman, etc.

If you are celebrating Chinese New Year, allow the young children to feel the noodles, create pictures with the noodles – even eat them.

Age group 2–4 years

At this age children should be more familiar with their everyday surroundings. They will now benefit from exploring things in more detail.

Encourage them to dig in the garden, to collect leaves, conkers, stones and talk about their properties.

If possible visit the supermarket before turning the home corner into a shop. While you are there point out how a machine reads how much things cost.

Figure 6.4 'Grow beans or sunflowers and plot their growth.'

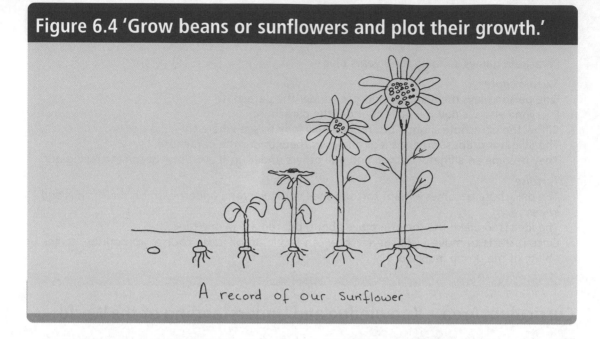

A record of our sunflower

Make maps of the area around the nursery. Discuss how the children get to the nursery.

When doing creative activities, encourage the children to think about different ways of using materials – printing with different things like cotton reels, leaves and combs and making rubbings from tree bark and bricks.

When providing construction materials, still allow experimentation but begin to encourage children to plan, perhaps following a picture.

Investigate 'growing' by planting seeds.

Introduce technology using tape machines, headphones, telephones and computers.

Figure 6.5 Different ages will work together to achieve an aim

Age group 4–8 years

Children should now begin to understand the written word, so they will benefit more from using books and CD-ROMs to gain information. If possible have books in other languages to show the different ways in which words can be written.

Encourage thinking about time-scale, e.g. past and present, by having a project about families – pictures of themselves, parents and grandparents.

Look at how toys have changed over the years – from rag dolls to robots that can be programmed.

A road safety project could include how traffic lights work and what traffic signs mean. This could lead to looking at other ways we use signs.

Investigate what local shops sell – where does the produce come from?

While out, consider how we dispose of our litter – what is the recycling system in your area?

Raise awareness of other cultures by looking at different cooking processes using different utensils.

Age group 9–11 years

Most children of this age group find the world around them exciting and an adventure. They contrast between calm and confident and out of control and unsure depending on the situation. They are finding out about their bodies and enjoy sharing information with friends rather than adults.

The main changes in their development include their ability to reason and this helps with games that have rules. They are also more co-ordinated. Children and young people of this age may join football, rounders or table tennis teams. They love to be picked for group activities such as sports day events at school, or plan to achieve badges and certificates in local groups and clubs. This is the age when being a member of the 'gang' is very important. They also like to have time to organize their own activities and games. However, they may recognize that other children are better at some things and feel that they cannot compete. This can affect their confidence and their willingness to take part. Adults need to give encouragement and support.

Figure 6.6 At age 10 will concentrate well to achieve a task

Figure 6.7 At 11 enjoy devising dance routines

Age group 11–13 years

Young people at this age can be quite unsure of themselves. Their lives are being affected by huge changes. Their bodies will be evolving rapidly. They will have the upheaval of leaving a small primary school where they were well known, and the biggest, to a much larger secondary where the routine is very different and they are 'very small fish'. They may also be split from friends who are going to a different school, just at the time when friends have become such an important influence on their lives.

Youth clubs will provide an opportunity to mix with peer groups, to play sports and games and generally enjoy themselves.

Competitive games are popular: football, snooker, pool, darts, volleyball, dance competitions, basketball, rugby and many more informal games that young people will devise for themselves.

Workers need to realize that these young people will want to make their own choices about how they spend their leisure time. Some will participate in a number of sporting activities, while others spend hours downloading music on to an iPod.

Age group 13–16 years

Young people of this particular age may seem more reserved, quieter, and easily embarrassed in family situations. Their moods can change suddenly and they want to be more independent and be allowed to take risks. They may enjoy the challenge of camping away from home; they will love lighting fires and organizing their own food. Some young people will enjoy activities that require new skills such as skiing or abseiling. However, some young people may just enjoy a quiet space to unwind, play computer games, read magazines and chat after they finish homework.

Older adolescents may like taking responsibility for younger children. They may enjoy sorting out teams, fixtures and competitive games.

Figure 6.8 Very good eye–hand control at age 13

They will have their own ideas and these may be different from their parents'. As a worker with this age group one of the most important roles you can take is to be an adult who is able to listen and be sensitive to their needs. You will have the skills to assess risk so that you can provide an exciting, challenging environment.

Although not strictly an activity you can also provide a platform for young people to discuss important issues that they need to be aware of. They do need information about drugs, alcohol and sex and this can be done more informally than school, with less family tensions than at home.

Special Needs Awareness

Since the 1981 Education Act there has been a change in attitudes and assumptions about children with special needs. There have been moves towards much more integration and inclusiveness within the care and education settings. This was reiterated in the 1994 Code of Practice, which states that schools must create a positive partnership with parents, draw up a special educational needs policy and appoint a Special Educational Needs Co-ordinator (SENCO).

The 2001 SEN Code of Practice, which at present only relates to England, outlines seven key principles when working with children. They relate to the ways that parents should be involved in the partnership, recognizing the importance of their contribution and the need to have their wishes respected.

The 2004 Education Act continues with the theme for promoting the integration of special needs children into mainstream nurseries and schools. The terminology used refers to 'inclusive care and education', which recognizes that care and education cannot be separated.

The Act also incorporates the ideas that underpin 'Every child matters'. This document came about as a result of asking children and young people what they wanted from education, health, social welfare, etc., which revealed that all children wanted to:

- be healthy;
- stay safe;
- enjoy and achieve;
- make a positive contribution;
- achieve economic well-being.

As an early years worker you may well look after children with a range of special needs. You will need to carry out observations and work closely with parents/carers to plan how best to work with them.

Throughout infancy and childhood, child health promotion and surveillance programmes should be offered. Observation of children by family doctors, health visitors, nursery and school staff and parents can identify, at an early age, those who may have special needs. Appropriate help can often limit or reverse the difficulties or delay. (Dare and O'Donovan, 1997)

All activities should be appraised in order to consider how they could best accommodate the child's needs. This may mean adapting the physical environment for a child in a wheelchair or with a visual impairment, or looking at where they have reached on the developmental continuum in order to simplify or extend the activity.

REFERENCES

Dare, A. and O'Donovan, M. (1997) *Good Practice in Caring for Young Children with Special Needs.* Leckhampton: Nelson Thornes.

DfES (2002) *Birth to Three Matters.* London: DfES.

CHAPTER SEVEN

Developmental Milestones from Birth to 16

In previous chapters we have discussed how to carry out observations in different formats. We considered how the knowledge we gained could help children and young people to progress, and how the activities we provided could lead a child or young person forward. As part of the process of evaluation it was also pointed out that it is necessary to compare your findings with what we expect children and young people to be doing at different stages.

In Chapter 3 there are references to the works of developmentalists, theorists and the standards of the National Curriculum. There are many books written about the sequence of children's and young people's development, and it is important that you read a good selection. However, to enable you to start your observations, we have included a summary of the main developmental milestones up to the age of 16 years to which you can refer.

As stated many times, however, you must take into consideration the fact that children and young people differ in quite normal ways. All children and young people follow the same sequence of growth and development, but the rate varies between individuals. Each aspect of development can be affected by the environment in which the child/young person is placed and the experiences they encounter. No two children/young persons, even though living in the same material environment, will have exactly the same experiences, or will be affected by them in exactly the same way. Every person is unique and will progress at their own individual rate. However, if we want to provide the best opportunities to encourage the child's/young person's development, we must know broadly what to expect of them at each stage, so that we can provide the right environment. In this way we would hope to meet their needs and allow them to reach their full potential.

The child/young person is a whole person and all aspects of development go on simultaneously, but observations often concentrate on one area, so the age-related guide that follows is arranged under five headings: physical, intellectual, language, social and emotional. For ease of writing and reference the stages from the age of 3 to 7 years are arranged in whole years. However, the reader will need to bear in mind that we would not expect a child of 4 years 1 month to be at the same stage as a child of 4 years 11 months. Nought to 3 years is divided into smaller sections, as development is particularly rapid in these years. Eight to 16 years development is in larger sections, e.g. 8 to 11, 11 to 14 and 14 to 16 years.

Students often hope to find that the behaviour they observe will be referred to in exactly the same language in the reference book. This is not always the case – you may need to adapt the skill to another situation. For example, if the reference book mentions a child's ability to complete a puzzle you might also compare a child's ability to fit other pieces together, such as a train layout or Lego construction following a picture clue. You may also need to look backwards or forwards in the milestones to see if the skill has been mentioned in a different age group. This is particularly true in the physical section, where abilities cannot be mentioned every time.

Lastly, it must be noted that most of the observations and developmental stages are based on the writers' experiences of working with children in England. There will inevitably be variations in the cultural and social expectations of children and young people which may affect the way in which they develop. The knowledge for compiling the stages comes from observing children and young people over many years and reflects many different experiences. They are not based on any standardized results, such as those used to compile growth charts or Sheridan's (1997) developmental stages, but they obviously reflect some of the learning undertaken by the writers during their own training and work. This is particularly true for Carole Sharman, whose work as a Health Visitor involved screening children for any developmental delay using, first, Mary Sheridan's guidelines, and then the Denver Developmental Screening Test. The Denver guidelines were standardized in the USA, as the name suggests, and do reflect the different ethnic groups that make up the population. All the authors have worked with nursery and school-age children before teaching on Nursery Nurse/Early Years/Teaching Assistant courses in further education and they continue to observe children and young people when visiting student placements/workplaces. In the light of the new Care, Learning and Development NVQ standards the older age groups have now been observed. The guidelines therefore reflect as up-to-date practice as possible.

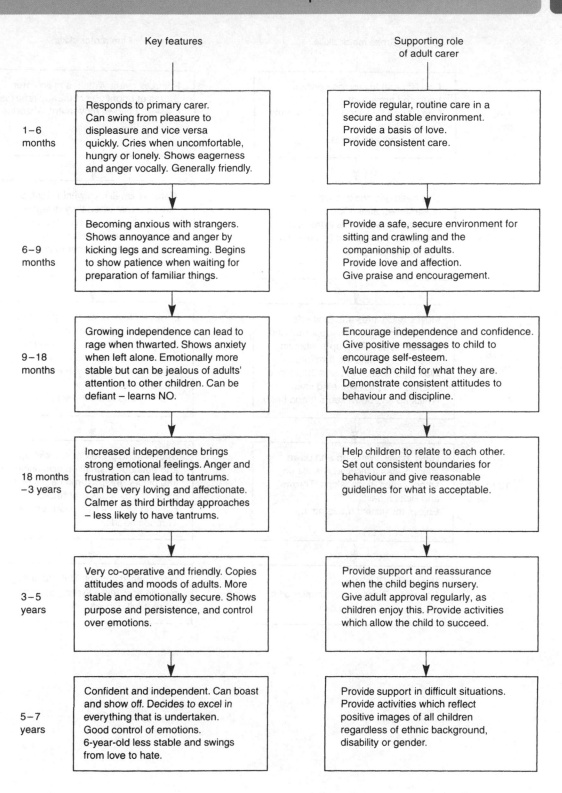

Key features	Supporting role of adult carer
1–6 months Responds to primary carer. Can swing from pleasure to displeasure and vice versa quickly. Cries when uncomfortable, hungry or lonely. Shows eagerness and anger vocally. Generally friendly.	Provide regular, routine care in a secure and stable environment. Provide a basis of love. Provide consistent care.
6–9 months Becoming anxious with strangers. Shows annoyance and anger by kicking legs and screaming. Begins to show patience when waiting for preparation of familiar things.	Provide a safe, secure environment for sitting and crawling and the companionship of adults. Provide love and affection. Give praise and encouragement.
9–18 months Growing independence can lead to rage when thwarted. Shows anxiety when left alone. Emotionally more stable but can be jealous of adults' attention to other children. Can be defiant – learns NO.	Encourage independence and confidence. Give positive messages to child to encourage self-esteem. Value each child for what they are. Demonstrate consistent attitudes to behaviour and discipline.
18 months –3 years Increased independence brings strong emotional feelings. Anger and frustration can lead to tantrums. Can be very loving and affectionate. Calmer as third birthday approaches – less likely to have tantrums.	Help children to relate to each other. Set out consistent boundaries for behaviour and give reasonable guidelines for what is acceptable.
3–5 years Very co-operative and friendly. Copies attitudes and moods of adults. More stable and emotionally secure. Shows purpose and persistence, and control over emotions.	Provide support and reassurance when the child begins nursery. Give adult approval regularly, as children enjoy this. Provide activities which allow the child to succeed.
5–7 years Confident and independent. Can boast and show off. Decides to excel in everything that is undertaken. Good control of emotions. 6-year-old less stable and swings from love to hate.	Provide support in difficult situations. Provide activities which reflect positive images of all children regardless of ethnic background, disability or gender.

Figure 7.1 Emotional development

Gross motor skills | Fine motor skills

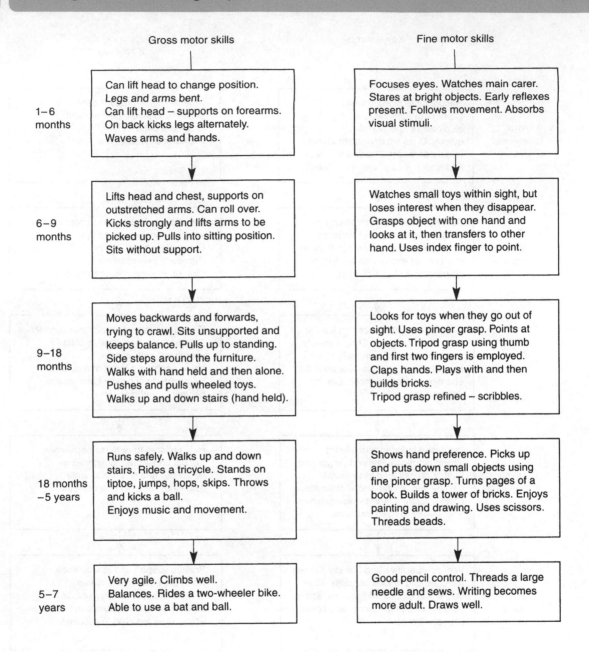

1–6 months

Gross motor skills:
Can lift head to change position.
Legs and arms bent.
Can lift head – supports on forearms.
On back kicks legs alternately.
Waves arms and hands.

Fine motor skills:
Focuses eyes. Watches main carer.
Stares at bright objects. Early reflexes present. Follows movement. Absorbs visual stimuli.

6–9 months

Gross motor skills:
Lifts head and chest, supports on outstretched arms. Can roll over.
Kicks strongly and lifts arms to be picked up. Pulls into sitting position.
Sits without support.

Fine motor skills:
Watches small toys within sight, but loses interest when they disappear.
Grasps object with one hand and looks at it, then transfers to other hand. Uses index finger to point.

9–18 months

Gross motor skills:
Moves backwards and forwards, trying to crawl. Sits unsupported and keeps balance. Pulls up to standing.
Side steps around the furniture.
Walks with hand held and then alone.
Pushes and pulls wheeled toys.
Walks up and down stairs (hand held).

Fine motor skills:
Looks for toys when they go out of sight. Uses pincer grasp. Points at objects. Tripod grasp using thumb and first two fingers is employed.
Claps hands. Plays with and then builds bricks.
Tripod grasp refined – scribbles.

18 months –5 years

Gross motor skills:
Runs safely. Walks up and down stairs. Rides a tricycle. Stands on tiptoe, jumps, hops, skips. Throws and kicks a ball.
Enjoys music and movement.

Fine motor skills:
Shows hand preference. Picks up and puts down small objects using fine pincer grasp. Turns pages of a book. Builds a tower of bricks. Enjoys painting and drawing. Uses scissors.
Threads beads.

5–7 years

Gross motor skills:
Very agile. Climbs well.
Balances. Rides a two-wheeler bike.
Able to use a bat and ball.

Fine motor skills:
Good pencil control. Threads a large needle and sews. Writing becomes more adult. Draws well.

Figure 7.2 Physical development

	Language development	Promoting language development	Cognitive development
1–6 months	Cries are voluntary. Begins to smile. Gurgles at carer. Moves eyes towards sound. Raises head toward sound. Shouts to attract attention. Begins to babble and repeat sounds.	Respond to baby's interactions. Talk to baby. Soothe baby with conversation and singing.	Baby is learning through senses. Sensory-motor period. Explores and discovers with mouth.
6–9 months	Plays around with sounds. Laughing and gurgling become stronger. Begins to enjoy music. Babbling increases. Begins to recognize own name. Understands simple words.	Listen to baby trying to communicate. Introduce picture books, sing simple nursery rhymes and finger/toe songs.	Continues to explore with mouth, and now fingers.
9–18 months	Babbling reflects speech intonation. Tries to imitate simple words. Begins to point. Awareness of words associated with people. Vocabulary starts to develop but understands more than can say.	Sing songs, rhymes and play simple games, e.g. Peek-a-boo, Ride-a-cock-horse. Read short stories regularly. Encourage the use of books. Encourage conversation.	Child sees the world from their point of view; egocentric. Begins to realize that objects exist when they are out of sight. Learning through 'trial and error'.
18 months –3 years	Vocabulary increases – names familiar objects. Begins to repeat words and sentences. Rapid increase in vocabulary. Two-word phrases. Personal pronouns used. Sentences longer but uses telegraphic speech. Listens to stories.	Regularly read and tell stories. Use open-ended questions. Give the child opportunity to verbalize. Listen carefully. Encourage child-to-child conversations.	Begins to make order of things through use of words. Child is still egocentric. Thinking is still connected to concrete objects and what is seen. Begins to predict what is going to happen.
3–5 years	New words picked up quickly. Longer sentences – more like adult speech. Pronouns used correctly. Language used to repeat past experiences. May over–generalize word endings. Tells long stories. Asks many questions.	Provide activities to encourage language. Use books from around the world. Listen to children. Continue to use open-ended questions.	Reasoning often illogical. Thoughts often 'black and white'. Begins to classify objects and gain concept of number.

Intellectual development

Figure 7.3 Intellectual, language and cognitive development

Social development

Making relationships

1–6 months
Responds to primary carer by smiling. Looks at human faces. Most content when near carer/mother. Watches movement of other people.

6–9 months
Turns in direction of mother's voice. Upset when separated from primary carer. Relates to wider family members.

9–18 months
Increased fear of strangers. May begin to use 'comforter'. Offers objects to friendly adults. Plays Peek-a-boo with known family.

18 months –3 years
Not so co-operative with adults for dressing and feeding. Often says 'no'. When hurt or overtired shows increased dependence on mother/main carer. Enjoys sharing experiences.

3–5 years
Has own sense of identity. Plays with one or two children then in larger groups. Shows concern for 'hurt' children. Can take turns. Still needs adult comfort and support.

5–7 years
More confident and independent. Moves away from adult dependence.

Socialization

Senses presence of mother/main carer. Smiles now to most other people. Babbles and gurgles and enjoys vocalizing in turns.

Watches and is interested in everything around. Begins to relate differently to known family than to strangers.

Increased fear of strangers. Claps hands to nursery rhymes. Enjoys sounds and tries to copy adults. Needs mother's approval before greeting strangers.

Tries to join in when sung to. Remains self-centred and shows pleasure in own possessions. Copies adults with purpose.

Talks freely to self and others. Make-believe play important – own experience and others'. Groups of children centre on activity.

Content to play alone for long periods. Aware of acceptable behaviour and manners.

Development of social skills

Responds to primary carer. Watches human faces. Smiles at most people and willing to be nursed by anyone. Gurgles and responds to being handled and spoken to.

Holds arms up to be lifted. Generally friendly, but fears strangers and watches them carefully.

Increased fear of strangers but takes cue from main carer's reaction to new situations. Shows interest in everything.

Plays alone but likes to know familiar adult is near. Tries to be independent. Plays beside another child but not with them.

Responds and talks to people. Plays contentedly with one or two children. Plays with groups of children – sometimes with one special friend.

Prefers rivalry games to team games.

Figure 7.4 Social development

8–11 years old

Key indicators

Supporting role of adult

Physical
Rapid development.
Increased muscle strength.
Agile and well co-ordinated.
Good fine motor skills.

Physical
Encourage participation in physical activities such as dance, swimming and gymnastics. Make time for activities such as skipping, running and jumping.

Intellectual
More sophisticated verbally and mentally.
Range of interests developing.
Able to think more logically.
More capable of using argument.

Intellectual
Support and encourage to organize their time when undertaking activities such as homework. Encourage after-school clubs and activities.

Social
Friends usually of same gender.
Quest for independence.
Often beginning to show loyalty to the group.

Social
Provide clear rules and guidelines for behaviour. Encourage basic social rules such as sharing and co-operation. Listen to children and praise.

Emotional
Can resent adult restrictions.
Achievement important and failure can upset the child and cause loss of confidence.
Onset of puberty can cause emotional changes.

Emotional
Demonstrate affection and support. Encourage children to talk about their feelings.

Figure 7.5

11–14 years old

Key indicators

Physical
Growth spurts and physical changes due to puberty.
Girls – breast growth, body hair, menstruation.
Boys – growth of testes and penis, body hair, voice deepening.

Intellectual
Starting to have their own ideas about things.
Testing verbal fluency and abstract thoughts but not as communicative as when younger although will talk about issues concerning them.
Can plan ahead.

Social
Peers more influential.
Gaining security from group acceptance.
Increased interest in the opposite sex.

Emotional
Emotions can fluctuate wildly.
Becoming more self-reliant and asserting, but can be hypersensitive and embarrassment is normal. Can be defiant.

Supporting role of adult

Physical
Encourage physical activities and exercise to strengthen developing muscles.
Encourage healthy eating and sufficient amount of sleep.

Intellectual
Take an interest in what the young person is doing and maintain good relationships if possible. Avoid criticism.
Create opportunities to undertake activities that will challenge intellectually.
Encourage reading for enjoyment and study.

Social
Encourage debate. Listen.
Be consistent with rules and boundaries.
Encourage involvement with the community and out-of-school activities.

Emotional
Be generous with praise and help to persevere. Be affectionate and loving.
Provide space to allow to be on their own.

Figure 7.5 continued

14–16 years old

Key indicators	Supporting role of adult
Physical Boys grow rapidly and are often more awkward. Most boys' voices will have broken and some will be shaving facial hair. Girls are usually physically mature, with all reproductive organs developed and regular menstruation.	**Physical** Encourage physical activities such as swimming, and provide opportunities for activities that are more physically challenging such as windsurfing, rock climbing and water skiing. Encourage a healthy, balanced diet.
Intellectual More interests and a greater awareness of the world. Can think independently and make decisions. Able to think about possibilities that are not directly observed. Plans well and able to write quickly and legibly.	**Intellectual** Give honest answers to questions. Provide opportunities for the development of leadership skills and encourage debate. Help to explore the world of work. Encourage involvement with out-of-school activities. Try not to over-criticize appearance!
Social Friends are most important and their approval is sought. Friendships are more lasting and intimate. More sociable when wants to be.	**Social** Be aware of negative peer pressure. Encourage participation in contributing to set rules, goals and boundaries.
Emotional May put energies into intimate relationship, and become depressed if there is a breakup. Less self-absorbed and has a greater ability to compromise. More tolerant and composed.	**Emotional** Give support and affection. Praise regularly. Try to avoid arguments about appearance. Allow time to be with peers.

Figure 7.5 continued

The neonate

At birth infants are dependent on an adult to meet their needs for protection, love and food. Their movements are mainly reflex, although the latest research suggests babies are able to 'copy' certain gestures soon after delivery. They communicate their needs by crying.

Physical development

The body of a full-term baby is rounded and on average weighs 3.4 kg. Length is around 45 to 50 cm. The head is large in proportion to the body.

- When the baby is pulled to a sitting position the head falls back, but held upright under the arms the shoulders support the head for a few seconds before giving way. Placed on their stomachs (prone) the head turns to one side and the legs are drawn up under the abdomen.
- On their back (supine) the head is on one side and the arm on that side is extended. If the head is turned round to the other side that arm will extend (tonic neck reflex).
- Other reflexes present at birth, but that will disappear in six to eight weeks are Moro – the falling/startle reflex, rooting, sucking, grasping, walking and stepping.
- Sight – turns to light, sharp visual field 25 to 30 cm. Opens eyes when held upright and blinks at any sound or movement.
- Hearing is acute – turns to sound, responds to voice, especially female pitch and recognizes mother's or carer's voice when one week old.
- Smell and taste sensitive – recognizes mother's milk, responds to nice and nasty smells.
- Touch response is strong – many of the reflexes are a response to touch.
- Babies will often be comforted by touch and it is thought to be a major factor in the bonding process. This has implications for premature babies kept in incubators.
- Sleeps about 21 hours a day.

Intellectual development

Sucking gives pleasure and babies learn to recognize the sights and sounds of feeding.

- Has been shown to concentrate on faces and imitate – yawning and tongue poking.
- Responds to primary carer.
- Can swing from pleasure to displeasure and vice versa quickly.
- Shows eagerness and anger vocally.

Language development

Communicates needs by crying, which can often be distinguished by main carer as indicating hunger, tiredness, boredom, pain or discomfort.

- Grunts and smiles with satisfaction.
- Will often 'still' to a continuous, moderately loud, adult voice.
- Uses movement and own activity to explore their senses.

Social and emotional development

Depends mainly on interaction with family or carers to develop early attachments.

- Responds to nursing but does not like to be overhandled.
- Likes to sleep, but very alert when awake.
- Expresses pleasure by using whole body movements, e.g. while feeding.

Supporting role of adult

Provide regular, routine care in a secure and stable environment.

- Provide a basis of love and consistent care.
- Talk quietly and affectionately to baby and give them a chance to respond.
- Talk to the baby with face-to-face contact.
- Encourage bonding with the baby's mother or main carer.

Three months old

Babies are awake for longer periods and are beginning to understand more about themselves and the wider environment. Their actions and language have become more deliberate.

Physical development

Actions are more controlled and purposeful. Early reflexes have disappeared.

- Supine, lies with head in mid-line and there is little or no head lag when pulled up to sitting.
- Held in the sitting position the back is straighter except in the lumbar region.
- Kicks very vigorously but if held in the standing position the legs tend to sag at the knees.
- Waves hand symmetrically and will bring hands together across the chest to hold a rattle momentarily.
- When placed in the prone position will lift up on to forearms to have a look round.
- Visually alert – follows a moving object around and will stare at a still object for a few seconds. Watches main carer, absorbs visual stimuli. Able to focus eyes on an object, and moves head to follow adult movement or a moving toy. Watches own hands very closely and plays with fingers. The defensive blink reflex is now present.
- Turns head and eyes to locate a sound but upset by very loud noises.
- May be sleeping through the night and awake for longer periods after a feed.

Intellectual development

Recognizes familiar sounds and objects, such as the bath running or feed arriving and shows excitement by kicking legs and vocalizing.

- Takes an interest in immediate environment including playthings.
- Has learned that calling out brings attention and relief.
- Generally friendly, responding well to primary carer.
- Baby is learning through senses. 'Sensory-motor' period described by Piaget.
- Explores and discovers with mouth.

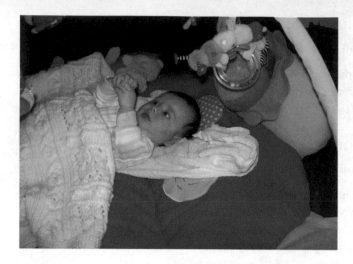

Figure 7.6 Waves hands symmetrically and will bring hands together across the chest

Language development

Vocalizes loudly, laughs.

Coos and squeals with pleasure.

Takes turns in conversations with adults, smiles in response to being talked to.

Social development

Responds to handling with smiles and gurgles.

Friendly towards any interested adult or child. Enjoys games with them.

Emotional development

Less self-centred and reacts more to the surroundings, but dislikes sudden loud noises and cries when uncomfortable or annoyed.

Demonstrates enjoyment in day-to-day routines such as bath time.

Enjoys being cuddled and being given attention.

Supporting role of adult

To offer reassurance and care, baby still very dependent on familiar adults.

To continue to provide regular, consistent, routine care and love in a secure and stable environment.

Provide colourful mobiles; sing nursery rhymes and action songs.

Encourage contact with other children and adults.

Respond to baby's interactions. Talk to baby.

Soothe baby with conversation and singing.

Six months old

Babies now have better control and begin to explore more with their hands. Better eye–hand co-ordination allows them to reach out and grasp objects. They are learning that they are separate from their environment.

Physical development

Laid on their back, they can raise head and lift legs to grasp hold of feet.

When placed on stomach lifts head and chest well off the ground, supporting self on flattened palms and outstretched arms.

Can sit with support and turn round to look at the surroundings.

Moves hands and arms purposefully and will hold out arms to be picked up.

When pulled into a sitting position will help by bracing the shoulders.

Held to stand, can support own weight and loves to bounce up and down.

Kicks strongly with alternating feet. Able to roll over from back to front.

Has a straight back if held standing or held sitting.

Picks up toys using whole hand (palmar grasp) and can pass from hand to hand.

Will reach out for a toy when offered one. Are visually alert.

Explores everything with the mouth.

Uses index finger to point.

First teeth may appear. Able to chew and take solids well.

Intellectual development

Beginning to react negatively to strange people or situations.

Will watch where a toy falls if it is within visual field but forgets if it disappears.

Beginning to understand cause and effect, e.g. rattle makes noise if shaken.

Smiles at own image in mirror. Will imitate for effect, e.g. coughing.

Language development

Uses voice tunefully, making sing-song vowel sounds or single or double syllables such as la-la, da-da, u-u, ga-ga, ah-ah.

Laughs, chuckles and squeals with delight or annoyance.

Babbles and repeats sounds and enjoys vocalizing in turns.

Begins to understand words such as 'mama', 'dada' and 'bye-bye'.

Social development

Sleeps less and wants more company to play with.

Often still friendly towards strangers but beginning to be shy or anxious when approached, especially if main carer is out of sight.

Most content when near carer/mother.

Watches movements of other people.

Babies begin to feed themselves with their fingers.

Emotional development

Still very reliant on main carer and familiar people and surroundings.

Beginning to show more independence but gets upset when mother or carer leaves.

Beginning to be aware of feelings of other people, e.g. laughing when others do.

Becoming more of a personality.

Shows annoyance and anger by kicking legs and screaming.

Begins to show patience when waiting for preparation of familiar things.

Supporting role of adult

Provide a safe, secure environment for sitting and crawling and the companionship of adults.

Encourage desire to crawl by placing toys just away from baby's reach.

Provide love and affection. Give praise and encouragement.

Listen to baby trying to communicate. Introduce picture books; sing nursery rhymes and finger/toe songs.

Nine months old

Babies at this age are now becoming mobile. Crawling, shuffling, creeping and rolling enables them to extend their world. Finer finger control allows detailed exploration of that world.

Physical development

Moving around the floor.

Pulls self up to stand, using furniture, people, etc. and will stand holding on. However, when lets go, falls backwards with a bump.

Held standing, will walk forward – one foot in front of the other.

Sits unsupported for long periods of time and can lean forward to reach a toy without over-balancing.

Uses a crude thumb and index finger (pincer) grasp to pick up small objects and pokes with index finger.

Tries to take the spoon when being fed. Finger-feeds well.

Intellectual development

Very interested in their surroundings. When exploring, shows great determination and curiosity.

Still examines things with the mouth.

Will search for toys that go out of sight as realizes they still exist.

Imitates clapping and waves bye-bye with some understanding of meaning.

Language development

Uses voice deliberately and will shout for attention.

Babbles tunefully: dad-dad-dad, mum-mum-mum. This is largely for babies' own amusement but also demonstrates an ability to recognize main carers.

Babbling increases and reflects speech intonation. Begins to recognize own name.

Understands simple words such as 'no' and 'bye-bye'.

Imitates sounds and converses in a two-way conversation.

Social development

Happy and sociable with familiar adults and children, but may be shy of strangers. This will be shown by clinging to carer, hiding the face and taking the cue from the main carer's reaction to new situations.

Shows interest in everything.

Attracts attention by shouting or crawling over and pulling clothes of an adult.

May play Pat-a-cake or Peek-a-boo with known family.

Emotional development

Babies have really become attached to their families and depend on them for reassurance.

Because they are secure in their love they have become more aware of who is a stranger.

Increasingly seeking independence, they will throw themselves backwards and stiffen in annoyance if they cannot do what they want.

Shows anxiety when left alone.

Supporting role of adult

Encourage independence and confidence.

Give positive messages to child and encourage self-esteem.

Demonstrate consistent attitudes to behaviour and discipline.

Encourage language development by singing songs, saying rhymes, playing simple games and looking at picture books.

One year old

The horizontal position of the new-born has now given way to the vertical position of the one-year-old, struggling to learn to walk. Use of language is growing and they are enthusiastic in experimenting with their limited adult's vocalizations.

Physical development

Sits very well and can sit up from lying down unaided. Usually crawling or bottom shuffling very fast.

Pulls to standing, using furniture, but still collapses with a bump on letting go.

Walks sideways on tiptoe around the furniture. Walks with hand held. May stand alone for a few seconds.

May crawl upstairs (average 13 to 14 months).

Picks up small objects with neat pincer grasp (between thumb and tip of index finger).

Feeding skills: can hold cup and drink with a little assistance. Holds spoon but unable to feed self yet.

Will help with dressing, e.g. holding out arm for sleeve.

May only need one sleep during the day.

Intellectual development

Explores objects with mouth less often.

Drops and throws toys and watches them fall, then looks in the correct area when they roll out of sight. Begins to realize that objects exist when they are out of sight.

Likes to look out of the window and watch cars, people, etc.

Beginning to show an interest in pictures in books. Knows own name and responds to it.

Imitates a great deal. Enjoys sounds and will experiment with toys that make a noise.

Child sees the world from their point of view: egocentric.

Language development

Babbles loudly, tunefully and incessantly.

Understands simple commands, e.g. come to mummy/daddy.

May say two or three words (nouns) with meaning, e.g. mummy, daddy, sibling or pet's name, but understands many more.

Awareness of words associated with people.

Social development

Inclined to be shy with strangers – likes to be able to see and hear a familiar adult.

Shows an increased fear of strangers, but are affectionate towards people they know.

May begin to use 'comforter'.

Enjoys an audience and will repeat acts that are laughed at.

Claps hands to join in nursery rhymes.

Emotional development

Capable of primitive affection and jealous of main carer's attention.

Emotionally more stable but can be jealous of adults' attention to other children.

Developing a degree of independence as mobility increases, but need to be able to explore and then return for security.

Demonstrate a growing need for independence in their struggle to feed themselves.

Growing independence can lead to rage when thwarted.

Supporting role of adult

Give encouragement to independence and confidence.

Praise and encourage child, be positive and encourage self-esteem.

Be consistent in regard to behaviour and discipline.

Value each child for what they are.

To encourage language development read short stories and picture books regularly, sing songs and rhymes, hold conversations with the child.

Provide activities to promote creative development such as large paint brushes, crayons, large sheets of paper.

Provide a stimulating environment, especially one to promote their sensory development.

Fifteen months old

The baby is a toddler now. They are usually walking and, although unsteady, are very proud of the fact. Their mobility and increasing curiosity make this period an exciting but often frustrating time.

Demands on their carer are increased as toddlers become more daring in their explorations. They have to learn self-discipline and adapt to social demands and this can result in negative behaviour over the next two years.

Physical development

Walks alone with feet wide apart, using arms outstretched to help balance.

Can get to feet alone and launch forward, but progress is limited by falling or bumping into furniture.

Lets self down by collapsing backwards but may fall forwards into crawling position.

Crawls upstairs and can kneel to play with toys.

Can push a large truck along but has no control over where it goes.

Picks up small objects with a precise pincer grasp.

Holds a crayon with a palmar grasp and makes a mark on the paper if shown.

Holds two building blocks and may put one on top of the other.

Assists with dressing. Can bring spoon to mouth and obtain some food before turning it over.

Not able to throw yet, so just drops (casts) toys.

Pushes and pulls wheeled toys.

Intellectual development

Less likely to explore with mouth now, using fingers instead.

Points at familiar toys and objects when asked.

Intensely curious about everything around – people, objects and events – likes going out for trips.

Does not associate dolls with being a baby – will carry them by an arm, leg or hair.

Still sees the world from their point of view – egocentric.

Realizes that objects still exist even when out of sight.

Learning through 'trial and error' – needs to see things happening.

Language development

Jabbers loudly and continuously with sounds becoming more complex.

Can say about two to six recognizable words but understands many more, e.g. will respond to simple requests and point to something they want. Words are mainly understood by main carer. They can have different meaning depending on what is happening.

Recognizes familiar songs, rhymes and TV tunes and will attempt to join in.

Social development

Enjoys familiar company and loves fuss and attention.

Emotional development

Begins a period of emotional unsteadiness. May become negative and refuse to co-operate or do the opposite of what is asked.

Temper tantrums are not uncommon until the age of three.

Can be defiant, learns NO.

Very dependent on adults for reassurance.

Supporting role of adult

Give reassurance, encourage confidence and independence.

Give positive messages to the child to encourage self-esteem.

Continue to demonstrate consistency in discipline and attitudes to behaviour.

Encourage the use of books, read short stories on a regular basis, engage in conversation with the child and sing songs and rhymes.

Talk to child about activity and give time for a response.

Think about joining a mother and toddler group.

Provide activities to encourage creativity.

Eighteen months old

Children are gaining skill and confidence in movement (see Figure 7.7) and gradually adding to their vocabulary and understanding of the world. Emotionally they are still very dependent on the main carer and need a lot of affection and reassurance.

If they are allowed to be dependent at this stage they will develop the stability and feeling of self-worth that will enable them to be confident in the future.

Physical development

Walks well – no longer needing to hold out arms for balance.

Can stoop to pick up toys from the floor without falling over.

Walks upstairs holding on, but crawls down.

Pushes and pulls large wheeled toys (including walking backwards), but cannot steer round obstacles yet.

Climbs on to chair and then turns round to sit down.

Picks up small objects using pincer grasp.

Tripod grasp using thumb and first two fingers is employed and this becomes refined, e.g. when scribbling.

Clasps hands together.

Will hold a pencil and scribble and may be using preferred hand most of the time.

May have bowel control and begin to show an interest in potty.

Feeds self with a spoon and gets most of the food into the mouth.

Tries to undress – attempts to unfasten shoe and pull off socks.

Figure 7.7 Eighteen months old. Children are gaining skill and confidence in movement

Intellectual development

Very curious and determined to explore the environment with increasing understanding of where things belong.

Enjoys putting objects into containers and then tipping them out again.

Likes books with pictures of everyday objects in them and helps turn the pages, several at a time.

Imitates simple everyday activities, such as driving a car, using the telephone.

Can build a tower of three bricks or other everyday objects, such as cushions, cardboard boxes.

Can point to several parts of the body – nose, eyes, ears, etc.

Child is still egocentric – refers to themselves by name.

Language development

Chatters continuously while playing.

Uses 6 to 30+ words but understands many more, uses gestures with words.

Enjoys rhymes and tries to join in.

Attempts to sing and often seems to recognize TV themes.

Obeys simple requests, e.g. 'Go and get Grandma's car keys.'

Social development

Plays quite well alone (solitary play) but likes to be near a familiar adult or older brother or sister.

Plays alongside other children and seems to enjoy their company but does not play with them.

Enjoys songs, rhymes and books with adults (enjoys the individual attention).

Increased fear of strangers – needs carer's/mother's approval before greeting strangers.

Emotional development

Very dependent on familiar adult but likes to be independent at times, and this can cause conflict.

Can be defiant, may be frustrated, and might have an occasional temper tantrum.

Loves cuddles, fun games, tickling, hiding, chasing.

Supporting role of adult

Continue to encourage independence, confidence and self-esteem.

Be positive in your dealings with the child and value all children for what they are.

Be consistent in discipline and attitudes to behaviour.

Encourage language development by reading and sharing books, singing songs and rhymes and holding conversations with the child.

Provide activities with messy materials, e.g. dough, sand and water, and toys for make-believe play.

Two years old

At two years of age children take an enormous step forward in their intellectual development. They are learning to construct simple sentences that will be the basis on which they will develop verbal fluency in the third and fourth years. The child is still very curious, restless, and enjoys a great deal of motor activity but may be able to sustain very short periods of concentrated effort on an activity.

Physical development

Runs safely and is more efficient at avoiding obstacles.

Loves to climb over the furniture.

Walks up and down stairs – two feet to a stair.

Pushes and pulls large wheeled toys with a growing sense of in which direction they want them to go.

Throws a ball overhead and kicks it.

Sits on small tricycle but uses feet not pedals to move it.

Holds pencil in preferred hand using thumb and first two fingers – tripod grasp.

Scribbles circles and dots and imitates a vertical line with practice.

Spoon-feeds, drinks and chews efficiently.

Usually has control of bowels and may be dry in the day time.

Will have cut or will soon cut last tooth.

Puts on socks and shoes (not necessarily on the correct foot).

Intellectual development

Enjoys picture books and recognizes smaller details – turns pages more slowly.

Very curious about surroundings but has little understanding of common dangers.

Has no understanding of the need to defer immediate wishes – can't wait!

Engages in simple role or make-believe play.

Builds a tower of 6 or 7 blocks.

Can point to parts of body including knees, elbows, etc.

Begins to make order of things through use of words.

Child is still egocentric.

Thinking is still connected to concrete objects and what is seen.

Language development

Speech more recognizable to other than main carers.

Uses 150+ words and understands many more.

Puts two or more words together to form a phrase (telegraphic speech) or sentence.

Beginning to listen with interest to talk going on around them and responds to conversations directed towards them.

Refers to self by name and talks continually during play.

Consistently asks the names of objects and people in order to learn new words.

Rapid increase in vocabulary.

Joins in familiar rhymes and songs that they love to have repeated – a favourite word is 'again'.

Carries out instructions – when feels like it!

Social development

Follows carer around the house and imitates, consistently demanding attention.

Likes a response from an adult when has done something.

Plays contentedly near other children but not with them – parallel play.

Has no idea about sharing playthings or the adult's attention and will hold on to own possessions with determination.

Emotional development

Still in need of much attention, reassurance and love.

Very dependent on adults and jealous of attention given to others.

Beginning to say how they feel, but can be frustrated when not able to express themselves clearly. Anger and frustration can lead to tantrums.

Can be loving one minute and biting the next.

When hurt or overtired shows increased dependence on mother/main carer.

Supporting role of adult

Continue to demonstrate consistent attitudes to behaviour and discipline.

Help children to relate to each other and to express their feelings.

Continue to encourage independence, confidence and good self-esteem for the child.

Regularly read and tell stories to help language development.

Use open-ended questions and give child a chance to verbalize.

Encourage child-to-child conversations.

Take child outdoors and explore the natural environment.

Continue to provide activities/resources to promote creativity and role play.

Two-and-a-half years old

At two and a half the child is poised between dependence on a familiar adult and the ability to broaden horizons and spend some time with other adults and children at a pre-school/nursery.

Physically quite proficient, and able to be understood verbally for most of the time, they often still need the security of a familiar environment and should not be pushed too soon.

Physical development

Locomotor skills improving rapidly with practice.

    Walks upstairs and downstairs easily, two feet to a step.

    Can stand on tiptoe and is able to jump with two feet together.

    Runs well and stops efficiently, usually avoiding obstacles.

    Climbs nursery and garden apparatus, but may get stuck at the top.

    Can jump with two feet together from a low step.

    Throws and kicks a ball with some idea of where it will go.

    Eats skilfully with hands and utensils.

    Pulls down pants to use the toilet but needs assistance to pull them up.

    Usually dry in the day and maybe at night (very variable).

Intellectual development

Still little understanding of everyday dangers or the need to wait for something – including attention.

    Builds a tower of 7+ bricks.

    Enjoys picture books with minute detail in them.

    Holds a chubby pencil and will copy a horizontal line and circle.

    Recognizes self in photographs and knows own full name.

    More sustained role play – from life and TV characters.

    Plays meaningfully with miniature toys, e.g. farm animals and plastic cartoon characters, adding own commentary to the story.

    Child is still egocentric.

Language development

Uses 200 or more recognizable words.

    Continually asking 'What?' and 'Who?'

    Uses 'I', 'you' and 'me' correctly in conversation.

    Says a few nursery rhymes – more with the prompting of an adult.

    Sentences longer, but uses telegraphic speech.

    Listens and concentrates when having stories read.

Social development

Watches other children at play, occasionally joining in for a few minutes, but not really interested in sharing a game. Very happy to play with adults or older children who will give undivided attention and let the child win.

Emotional development

Still very dependent on adult.

    Throws tantrum when thwarted and is less easily distracted.

    Can be very loving and affectionate.

Supporting role of adult

Set out consistent boundaries for behaviour and give reasonable guidelines for what is acceptable. Help children to relate to each other.

Regularly read and tell stories.

Listen carefully and give the child opportunity to verbalize.

Use open-ended questions, encourage child-to-child conversation.

Introduce and play simple games of 'Let's Pretend'.

Three years old

The three-year-old is more agile and co-ordinated. Language is becoming an increasingly important tool – its social use is developing and if language development is retarded the child may find it difficult to make friends, join in group activities or obey fairly complicated instructions from an adult. All these things are necessary when the child begins to move out of the family circle and start pre-school/nursery, which is usual at this age. If the child is not able to use or understand language then anti-social behaviour may persist.

Physical development

Can jump with feet together, stand and walk on tiptoe and stand on one leg.

Uses climbing frames well.

Can steer round obstacles and corners while running and pushing toys.

Walks upstairs with alternating feet but still two feet to the stair coming down.

With practice can ride a tricycle or bicycle with stabilizers, kick a ball forcibly and hold and cut with scissors.

Can use a spoon and fork to eat if this is the family practice.

May be dry at night, but not unusual if they are not (especially boys).

Needs help with buttons when dressing.

Washes hands but needs help drying.

Able to use technical equipment such as computers if allowed.

Intellectual development

Shows some appreciation of differences between present and past and the need to wait for attention, sweets, ride on the swings, etc. (This is not highly developed and the three-year-old will still have difficulty understanding the need to take turns.)

Builds a tower of 9 bricks and copies a bridge made with them.

Enjoys floor play with bricks, boxes, etc. that can be used imaginatively.

Copies O, V and T shapes.

Draws a person with a head and usually some indication of one or two features.

Matches colours and may name two or three.

Enjoys painting for the sake of it with fingers or brush.

Plays inventive, imaginative games with make-believe people and objects.

Can count up to ten or more but has little appreciation of actual quantity beyond two or three.

Listens quietly to stories and loves to hear them over again.

Knows several rhymes and songs.

Can tell you their full name and sex.

Begins to predict what is going to happen next.

Language development

Extensive vocabulary that is usually intelligible even to strangers.

Uses pronouns and plurals but may over-generalize, e.g. 'sheeps'.

Initiates simple conversations by asking many questions: 'Who?', 'Why?', 'What?' and 'Where?'

Speech beginning to gain interest by changes of tone in the sentence.

Social development

General behaviour more co-operative – likes to help adults with activities.

Begins to join in games with other children and to share, but still needs to be in small groups.

Enjoys sharing experiences and family mealtimes.

Copies adults with a purpose, begins to help adults, e.g. tidying up.

Is interested in making friends and having friends.

Emotional development

Much steadier emotionally and so easier to manage.

Emotional maturity shows in friendliness, sociability and desire to please.

Affectionate towards carers, brothers and sisters and pets.

Feels more secure, so is able to share and play with others (this can revert if the child is unwell or feels less sure, e.g. new surroundings or unfamiliar adults).

Sometimes develop fears, e.g. frightened of the dark. This is because children are now more able to use their imagination.

Supporting role of adult

Be consistent with boundaries for behaviour and give reasonable guidelines for what is acceptable.

Help children to relate and co-operate with each other.

Continue to help language development by reading stories regularly, singing songs and rhymes, asking open-ended questions and listening to replies.

Encourage child-to-child conversations.

Provide a large range of playthings and creative materials.

Take child on visits to park, library, swimming pool.

Four years old

After the period of emotional and developmental stability around three years, children are again showing a 'see-saw' pattern of behaviour at the age of four. In struggling for the verbal, social and emotional confidence of the five-year-old the four-year-old can become 'a boastful, dogmatic and bossy showoff'. Their minds are lively, their imaginations vivid and their will strong, but their emotional unsteadiness shows itself in verbal impertinence and exaggeration.

Figure 7.8 Can ride bike using feet

Physical development

Very agile, can turn sharp corners when running, hop, walk on tiptoe, climb trees and ladders.

Climbs stairs and descends confidently one foot to a stair.

Good sense of balance.

Expert tricycle rider, using pedals and avoiding obstacles.

Increased skill in ball games – throws, catches, bounces and kicks with an idea of where the ball is going.

Good control of a pencil, which is held adult fashion.

Able to thread small beads on to a string and use scissors with practice.

Capable of washing and drying hands but often in too much of a hurry to complete the job well.

Can dress and undress except laces, ties and back buttons.

Intellectual development

Has an understanding of past, present and future time.

Builds tower of 10+ bricks and bridges. Can copy steps built of bricks.

Floor games very complicated, and construction play utilizes any available material.

Dramatic make-believe play can be sustained for long periods.

Copies cross, square and V, H, T and O shapes.

Draws a recognizable house and a person with head, possible trunk, legs and arms.

Beginning to name drawings and plan models before starting them.

Matches and names four colours correctly.

Recognizes and names circle, square and triangle.

Gives full name, address and age.

Able to recall and recount recent events.

Sometimes confuses fact and fantasy, but able to relate long stories.

Enjoys jokes.

Counts by rote up to 20 or more and may have understanding of number to 4 or 5.

Enjoys learning new skills such as computer games.

Reasoning often logical.

Thoughts often 'black and white'.

Language development

Speech intelligible and essentially grammatically correct.

May still have difficulty pronouncing w, f, th.

Continually asking questions: 'Why?', 'When?' and 'How?'

Loves new words and will invent them in order to tell a story or put an unknown into context, e.g. a picture of a camel is described as a 'horse with a hump'.

New words are picked up quickly.

Longer sentences, much more like adult speech.

Language used to repeat past experiences.

Social development

Likes the companionship of other children and adults but alternates between co-operation and conflict; however, understands the need to use words rather than blows.

Capable of sharing and taking turns but may cheat in order to win – this is very obvious in games such as Snakes and Ladders.

Shows sympathy for friends who are hurt.

Has own sense of identity.

Talks freely to self and others.

Make-believe play important – own experience and others'.

Emotional development

Is in a period of emotional unsteadiness, which is shown by cheekiness and impertinence rather than temper tantrums.

General behaviour more independent and self-willed, which can lead to conflict.

Can show sensitivity to other children and adults.

Has a developing sense of humour.

Supporting role of adult

Provide comfort, support and reassurance.

Give regular adult approval.

Provide activities that allow a child to succeed.

Demonstrate consistency in discipline and behaviour boundaries.

Provide activities to encourage language development, take child to library.

Continue to use open-ended questions and listen to children.

Provide space and opportunities for exercise.

Provide resources and activities to promote creative development.

Encourage children to use computer and to practise use of the mouse and some simple games.

Five years old

If raised in a supportive and stimulating environment five-year-olds are confident and have good self-control. Home will no longer satisfy their curiosity and desire for knowledge, and they are ready for the wider experience of school. Having achieved a measure of independence they are able to cope with the larger group and no longer require so much adult attention – although they will always thrive on praise and be proud of their achievements.

Physical development

Movements precise: runs lightly on toes and is able to walk along narrow line.
> Skilful in climbing, swinging and sliding, good balance, good co-ordination.
> Able to skip, hop and move rhythmically to music.
> Kicks and throws ball with considerable ability by focusing eyes on the objective.
> Good control of pencils, crayons and paint brushes.
> Well developed IT skills – video, computer.
> Uses a knife and fork with practice.
> Washes and dries face and hands, and can dress and undress (may need help with laces and ties).

Intellectual development

Draws recognizable people with head, trunk, features, arms and legs.
> Creates pictures – usually of people, houses, flowers and a large sun in the sky.
> Decides what to draw before commencing – although will often look across at neighbour and include something that they have drawn!
> Beginning to distinguish between truth and falsehood.
> Enjoys games with rules. May still attempt to 'cheat to win' but has an awareness of 'not fair'.
> Capable of colouring neatly and staying within the line.
> Names at least four colours.
> Can name and draw circle, square, rectangle and triangle.
> Writes a few letters – can often write own name in capital letters.
> Counts fingers on one hand with the index finger of the other.
> Loves to be read or told stories, which will often be acted out later in a complicated dramatic play.
> Shows a definite sense of humour and loves telling 'jokes'.
> Understands the need for tidiness but requires constant reminders to be tidy.
> Realizes that clock time has a relationship to the daily routine of events.
> Begins to classify objects and gain concept of number.

Language development

Speech fluent and grammatically correct.
> Loves new words and learns songs quickly.
> Constantly asking the meaning of new words, especially abstract words.
> Recognizes some written words and begins to write a few.
> Tells long stories, asks many questions.

Figure 7.9 At 4 years very agile – good sense of balance

Social development

Ready to mix with a wider group and to choose friends.

Proud of achievements and possessions.

Co-operative with friends most of the time and understands the need for rules.

Protective towards younger children and pets and shows concern if they are upset.

Plays in larger groups of children or plays contentedly with one or two children – often has one special friend.

Groups of children centre on one activity.

Understands social rules of how to greet others.

Will often help other children in distress.

Emotional development

Generally more sensible and controlled, more stable and emotionally secure.

Independent and ready to cope with challenges but needs praise and encouragement in order to progress.

Shows purpose and persistence, and control over emotions.

Supporting role of adult

Give adult approval regularly.

Set and maintain boundaries for behaviour, clearly explaining these to the child.

Provide activities to encourage language development.

Use books from around the world.

Continue to use open-ended questions and listen to children.

Encourage child to learn to swim, ride a bicycle and to join in games and activities that are non-stereotypical, e.g. girls playing football, boys cooking or skipping.

Six years old

Physically children continue to mature and refine their control of movement. Growth rates slow down. Emotionally the child is entering another period of upheaval. Between the ages of five and seven there is a major change in the way children think and feel and the six-year-old may experience difficulties in maintaining balance in their emotional behaviour. There are often swings of mood, periods of frenzied activity, and nightmares are not unusual. However, we can harness these energies by interesting children in new ideas and objects and encouraging them to explore and learn.

Physical development

Constantly 'on the go'. Rush about and often slam into things. However, the body is well co-ordinated, agile and strong, and eye and hand work together so that bat and ball games are more successful. Girls and boys are equally boisterous, but their energies are often channelled into cartwheels and dance for the girls, and wrestling for the boys.

Boys will often 'play' fight – this can end in tears as they do not know when to stop.

There will of course be cultural and social differences that will shape how boys and girls are expected to act.

All this dashing about makes children tired but they hate to give in and rest.

The child is beginning to lose first teeth as the second ones come through.

Children are very agile, climb and balance well and can ride a two-wheeled bicycle without stabilizers.

They have very good pencil control; writing becomes more adult and they can draw well.

Can thread a large needle and sew.

Intellectual development

Easily distracted because of physical energy, so learning is best channelled into exploratory methods where possible. The mind is very active and the child will move easily from one activity to another, but the six-year-old will complete a task on another day.

Decisions are not made as quickly as before, as more thinking is required – this shows increased maturity in weighing up the possibilities.

Draws more realistic and complicated pictures and begins to fill in the colour.

Interested in learning to read, and loves stories.

Has a better understanding of number symbols and enjoys games such as dominoes.

Has a concept of number, and beginning to develop a concept of time, distance, volume and measurement.

Is interested in basic scientific principles.

Language development

The six-year-old is an incessant chatterer, so enjoys oral work, but language now widens to include reading, writing and tapes, etc. There has been a great deal of research undertaken into the best method of teaching children to read. There does not appear to be any easy answer, but it can only be a help if we surround the child with all forms of language and demonstrate a love of it ourselves.

The six-year-old talks confidently and fluently and is able to pronounce most of the sounds of their own language.

Listens to stories, but also now enjoys reading them.

Social development

A difficult period as friendships form and dissolve rapidly.

Child often plays better with one friend rather than two.

Although not always the case boys are more likely to fight and girls to use verbal taunts when they fall out. 'You're not coming to my party' is often heard.

Children love parties and social functions at this age but it can be a traumatic time.

The six-year-old is eager for praise and recognition and would always like to win.

Attention from teacher/parent will spur them on, but they sometimes find correction difficult to accept.

Aware of acceptable behaviour and manners.

More confident and independent.

Emotional development

Because of their increased mental ability children are able to see that there are many sides to a question. This can make them hesitant, indecisive and frightened.

The six-year-old is very dependent on adults for direction and guidance.

Stress often shows as nightmares, which can be frightening.

Capable of bouts of strong verbal and physical temper but can also be very caring and considerate.

Can swing from love to hate.

Supporting role of adult

Provide support in difficult situations.

Give praise and recognition.

Provide activities that reflect positive images of all children regardless of ethnic background, disability or gender.

Provide opportunities for vigorous exercise.

Continue to encourage language skills by providing opportunities for writing, reading and listening, but do not continually correct grammatical mistakes.

Surround child with all forms of language.

Seven years old

The seven-year-old is a clear thinker and a steadier personality capable of long periods of concentrated effort. However, the child is moving from the pre-operational way of thinking into the concrete operational (Piaget). This means that they are able to categorize in various ways which may lead to confusion at times. A seven-year-old is interested in reading, writing, talking, listening and playing games with rules.

They have a good sense of what is right and wrong.

Physical development

Less likely to rush about than the six-year-old.

Have increased stamina especially for activities such as swimming and gymnastics.

Will practise something many times in order to perfect the movement.

Good co-ordination means that they are better at bat and ball games, and often skilful in throwing and catching.

Are usually competent in their writing skills.

Intellectual development

Now in the concrete operational stage, which allows them to store, retrieve and reorganize experiences to fit them to new challenges.

Because they have an insight into conclusions they often rub out their work in an attempt to be right.

Enjoy experimenting with and manipulating new materials.

Begin to tell the time accurately.

Able to conserve number, e.g. they are able to know that there are 12 buttons whether they are spread out or close together.

Can use a computer keyboard and mouse for word processing.

Beginning to do simple mental arithmetic.

Enjoy learning about the environment and living creatures.

Are able to draw logical conclusions and understand cause and effect.

Language development

Uses language more in order to reason, but still shouts if thinks something is unfair.

Enjoys exciting stories being read, but also reads to self more. Likes books with strong heroes. Interested in words – likes poetry and able to write own stories.

Uses computer for word processing and tape recorders for recording own stories.

In the National Curriculum at Key Stage 1 children are learning to speak confidently and listen to what others have to say.

Children are beginning to write independently and with enthusiasm.

They use language to explore their own experiences and imaginary worlds.

Social development

Very self-aware – no longer likes to get changed with other children.

Becoming more aware of the needs and feelings of others and likes to help.

Moving away from dependence on family for reassurance – anxious to please the teacher and older friends.

Has a gang of friends – usually ready to join clubs.

Forms close friendships, usually with their own gender.

Independent in all washing, dressing and toileting skills.

Emotional development

Personality quite well established.

Still not a good loser.

Absorbs more than gives out, so appears quieter.

Has a growing sense of right and wrong.

Outbursts are rare – more likely to sulk if upset.

Can control emotions, often hiding their true feelings.

Are able to express feelings of wonder and awe especially over natural surroundings, plants and animals.

Because of increased ability to imagine what is likely to occur, may have fears about self in new situations. This can cause problems with the move to a new school.

Supporting role of adult

Encourage outdoor play and games such as skipping and hopscotch.

Provide materials and resources to promote creative development, e.g. collage materials, clay and other modelling media.

Encourage child to make up stories and preserve them in a written or recorded format.

Visit a theatre, make puppets and put on puppet show.

Undertake simple scientific experiments, and record findings.

Introduce children to the different religions and festivals celebrated, e.g. Diwali, Hanukkah, Ramadan.

Eight to eleven years old

Between the ages of eight and eleven there are changes that take place in all areas of development. There may be a big difference in physical size and intellectual ability between boys and girls. It is normal for boys to be shorter than girls at this age.

Girls may be displaying early signs of puberty. Most girls begin puberty between the ages of nine and thirteen, and boys between the ages of ten and sixteen. Achievement is becoming more important to the child. The onset of puberty can influence the way children socialize and affect their self-esteem. Friends are becoming more important.

Physical development

Girls are developing rapidly; they are growing taller than boys.

The girls' growth spurt is due to an increase in hormone production and will lead to a more curvaceous body, including developing breasts. Menstruation usually follows about two years later. By the age of eleven their body proportions are the same as adults'.

Girls and boys have increased muscle strength, are agile, well co-ordinated, and control their bodies well. They have good hand dexterity and can undertake detailed work such as needlework or woodwork.

Handwriting is becoming well formed.

Intellectual development

Verbal and mental abilities are becoming more sophisticated.

More of an independent thinker.

Develop a range of interests, e.g. art, music, gymnastics.

Child has moved from thinking in a self-centred way to being able to see situations from another person's point of view, and is beginning to understand the reasons behind other people's actions.

Ideas of right and wrong, fairness and justice are developing from simple to more complex ideas.

Ideas become less dependent on having experienced a situation, more able to deal with abstract ideas.

Is able to think logically about objects and events. (Piaget – concrete operational stage.)

Better understanding of mathematical relationships. Achieving conservation of number, mass and weight.

Is able to classify objects according to several features and can order them in series along a single dimension such as size.

Gaining a more accurate and realistic understanding of the world.

Becoming more capable of reasoned argument.

Able to remember well, are attentive and able to express their ideas.

Language development

Begin to discover the power of words and may resort to verbal put-downs with family and friends. Do not always realize how hurtful words can be.

Vocabulary has extended and children are effective in written and verbal communications, enabling them to use language appropriately according to the social situation.

Speech and written work use more complex sentences.

Written work is often long and complex by the age of eleven.

In the National Curriculum at Key Stage 2 children learn to change the way they speak and write to suit different situations, purposes and audiences. They read a range of texts and respond to different layers of meaning in them. They explore the use of language in literary and non-literary texts and learn how language works.

Most children are reading fluently and handwriting is well formed.

Social development

Friends are generally of the same gender, although interest is being shown in the opposite sex. Friendships can be clique, and if a child is excluded it can be upsetting for them.

Growing potential for social maturity is enhanced by the quest for independence and autonomy linked to a greater reliance on friends.

Friends give this age group an important sense of belonging, personal affirmation and increased confidence. Friendships can change rapidly but by the age of eleven usually have a 'best friend'.

Often are beginning to show loyalty to a group.

Emotional development

Child begins to question parental judgement. Can resent adult authority and restrictions on freedom.

Turns to friends for acceptance but can easily be upset when their approval is not given.

Achievement is important and failure will upset child, can easily lose confidence.

Very aware of any shortcomings and weaknesses and views them as making them different from friends.

Self-conscious, especially regarding physical development.

Dramatic emotional changes associated with puberty may be being experienced, especially by girls.

Get easily upset if criticized.

Supporting role of adult

Have clear rules and guidelines for behaviour, these should be discussed with child.

Aim for high and consistent standards and consistent methods of discipline.

Demonstrate affection and support, embrace chosen friendships.

Support and encourage child to organize their time when undertaking activities such as homework.

Encourage after-school clubs, hobbies and activities such as swimming, gymnastics, music. Discourage too much watching of television and playing computer games.

Praise good behaviour and listen to child's opinions and encourage them to talk about their feelings.

Eleven to fourteen years old

The pre-teenager (eleven- to twelve-year-old) is beginning to know their own mind, testing out verbal fluency and the abstract thinking process. Boys still remain behind in terms of physical development. By thirteen most girls are physically mature, but there are variations of when puberty begins and ends. Boys' growth spurt usually reaches its peak two years after the start of puberty. For both sexes, hormonal changes usually start before entering their teenage years. These years see intense physical, emotional and psychological changes. Often there is conflict between teenagers and their parents or carers.

Physical development

Growth spurts – a boy may grow 12 to 15 cm between the ages of thirteen and fourteen, girls' fastest growth is usually around the age of twelve.

In girls breast development is usually the first sign of puberty – at the age of ten or eleven.

This is followed by underarm and body pubic hair at the age of eleven to thirteen.

Menstruation usually begins between the ages of eleven to fourteen.

In boys the testes grow between the ages of eleven and twelve and the penis starts to lengthen before it thickens between twelve and thirteen years. Ejaculation begins about one year after the penis begins to lengthen – thirteen to fourteen years of age.

Boys' pubic hair starts developing from the age of eleven or twelve until the appearance of facial hair at thirteen to fifteen years of age.

Voice begins to deepen between the ages of fourteen and fifteen.

Intellectual development

Thinks logically about abstract propositions and tests hypotheses systematically. (Piaget – formal operational stage.)

  Is concerned with the hypothetical, the future and ideological problems.

  Will think out a problem and approach it logically and systematically.

  Will plan ahead and undertake any necessary preparation.

  Education is a dominant part of teenage life.

Language development

Not as communicative as when they were younger – teenagers often reply with monosyllabic answers to questions put by adults.

  Teenagers like to talk about issues that affect themselves or their friends. They will often have views on such issues as capital punishment, worries about the environment, miscarriages of justice and spiritual matters.

  The National Curriculum will be being taught in schools and eleven- to fourteen-year-olds will be in Key Stage 3. The areas being covered by the National Curriculum in English include speaking and listening, group discussion and drama; reading – including texts from different cultures and English literary heritage; writing – composition, planning and drafting, punctuation, spelling, handwriting and standard English and language structure.

  Pupils are developing confidence in speaking and writing for public and formal purposes.

  They are also developing their ability to evaluate the way language is used.

  They read classic and contemporary texts and explore social and moral issues.

Social development

Teenagers beginning to move away from parents/carer towards their peers.

  Less concerned about adult approval, friends become more influential.

  Gain security from group acceptance and follow peer group dress and behaviour codes.

  Interested in the opposite sex, but likely to be shy.

  Mature twelve- or thirteen-year-olds look grown up but are still children underneath.

  Peer pressure can influence someone of this age to act older.

Emotional development

Can fluctuate between emotions, e.g. excitement to moodiness.

  Hormonal changes can lead to moodiness and emotional outbursts.

  Moving away from security of home and parents towards peers – subject therefore to all the whims of the peers and possible rejection.

  Can become hypersensitive, especially to issues relating to opposite sex.

  Embarrassment is normal, particularly becoming modest about their bodies and seeking privacy.

  Can be defiant and unco-operative – probably feeling uncertain and confused.

  Becoming self-reliant and asserting independence.

  Often feel misunderstood and want to be liked and accepted.

Supporting role of adult

Encourage debate, listen to teenager and give time for ideas and opinions to be discussed.

Avoid constant criticism, don't nag. Be generous with praise.

Take an interest in what the teenager is doing.

Try to maintain good relationships with teenager by handling them carefully and by getting a balance between allowing them to do things and being overprotective.

Encourage physical activities and exercise to strengthen developing muscles.

Encourage good sleeping and eating habits.

Be understanding of their desire to have some personal space.

Be consistent with rules and boundaries.

Encourage involvement with community and out-of-school activities.

Fourteen to sixteen years old

Physically these teenagers are turning into adults; boys grow rapidly during these years and may well overtake the girls. However, pubertal changes will continue at least until the age of seventeen. Boys' voices break between sixteen and seventeen years of age. Most girls have a regular menstrual cycle by the age of sixteen. A marked leaning towards some academic subjects is beginning to show. Serious consideration about a career and future role in life may be being thought about. Teenage self-preoccupation continues. More time is spent with friends of both sexes. There is a great desire to be accepted by peer group. Many teenagers are dating by this age and some may enter into very close and passionate relationships.

Physical development

Boys grow rapidly during this age. Appetite is usually large because of the rapid growth.

Boys often look and move awkwardly as they get used to their rapid increase in height – they may walk hunched over and look gangly. As his shoulders and muscles develop he will gradually change.

The penis and testes usually reach full adult size with mature sperm.

Facial hair is increasing and pubic hair is becoming thicker and darker.

It may be necessary for a boy to start shaving.

Girls are usually physically mature by sixteen years old. They have fully developed reproductive organs, may have reached adult height but could continue to put on weight.

Some girls may suffer from painful cramps or suffer from pre-menstrual bloating, moodiness and skin problems.

Boys and girls become more physically adventurous and take up activities such as rock climbing, water skiing and surfing.

Intellectual development

Specific intellectual interests such as languages, science or mathematics may begin to emerge. Between the ages of fourteen and eighteen young people choose their subjects and start to think about their future life choices.

This is a key period of learning and development.

May develop and be good at artistic subjects such as music, pottery or painting.

Can now think independently and make own decisions.

Able to think about possibilities that are not directly observable.

Able to plan well and organize their own thoughts.

Able to think and discuss issues that adults can be preoccupied with such as religion, spirituality, morality and politics.

Use imagination when problem solving.

Language development

Start to question things that had previously been taken for granted.

The National Curriculum at Key Stage 4 integrates 'speaking and listening', 'reading' and 'writing'. In Key Stage 4 young people learn to use language confidently in academic studies and for the world beyond school.

Young people learn to speak and listen confidently in a wide variety of contexts.

They learn to be flexible, adapting what they say and how they say it to different situations and people. They should be fluent and articulate in their use of spoken standard English. At Key Stage 4 young people are keen readers who can read many kinds of text and make articulate and perceptive comments about them.

In written language young people develop confidence in writing for a range of purposes. They develop their own distinctive style and recognize the importance of writing with commitment and vitality.

Social development

Friends are most important to this age group. More time will be spent with friends of both sexes; family is less important. Start to make lasting and more intimate friendships.

Accept own sexuality, form sexual relationships that involve feelings which have never been felt or dealt with before.

Experiment to find self-image they feel comfortable with.

More sociable, less shy as self-consciousness recedes.

Emotional development

May invest considerable emotional energy in a relationship, and may lose interest in other areas of life – including friends and schoolwork. This can lead to a difficult time for the young person when an intimate relationship breaks up. May become depressed.

Young people of this age are less self-absorbed and develop a greater ability to compromise, making them tolerant and more composed in themselves.

Supporting role of adult

Give honest answers to questions, especially about sex.

Give young person support, particularly if they become depressed – seek professional help.

Encourage young people to eat a balanced diet and have sufficient sleep.

Provide love and reassurance.

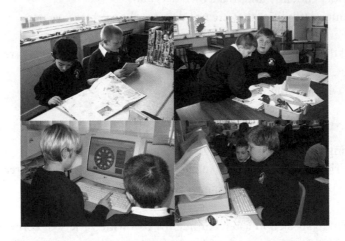

Figure 7.10 Friends are usually of the same gender

Be aware of negative peer pressure, e.g. encouraging experimentation with alcohol or other drugs.

Encourage some form of physical activity, e.g. swimming, wind surfing, water skiing. Do not overcriticize a young person's appearance.

Provide opportunities to develop leadership skills.

Encourage young person to contribute to the goals and boundaries for behaviour and such concerns as how late they are allowed to stay out.

Always give respect to this age group and listen to their ideas.

Help them to explore careers and the world of work.

Further Reading and Useful Websites

Further reading

Bee, H. (1992) *The Developing Child.* New York: Harper Collins.

Bruce, T. (2004) *Developing Learning in Early Childhood.* London: Sage.

Coleman, J. and Hendry, L. (1999) *The Nature of Adolescence* (3rd edn). London: Routledge.

Davenport, C. (1994) *An Introduction to Child Development* (2nd edn). London: Collins.

DfES/QCA (2003) *Foundation Stage Profile.* London: DfES.

Gross, R. (1992) *Psychology: The Science of Mind and Behaviour.* London: Hodder.

Lansdown, R. and Walker, M. (1996) *Your Child's Development from Birth to Adolescence* (2nd edn). London: Frances Lincoln.

Meggit, C. and Sunderland, G. (2000) *Child Development: An Illustrated Guide.* Oxford: Heinemann.

Nutbrown, C. (1999) *Threads of Thinking* (2nd edn). London: Paul Chapman.

Taylor, J. and Woods, M. (1998) *Early Childhood Studies: A Holistic Introduction.* London: Hodder.

Websites

www.everychildmatters.gov.uk
UK government website with full details of 'Every child matters: change for children' outlining and supporting the national approach to the well-being of children and young people from birth to age 19.

www.playbus.org.uk
UK website for the National Playbus Association, an umbrella organization supporting mobile community work across the United Kingdom.

www.pre-school.org.uk
UK website for the Pre-School Learning Alliance, a leading educational charity that specializes in the Early Years.

www.qca.org.uk
UK website for the Qualifications and Curriculum Authority, the body that regulates, develops and modernizes the curriculum, assessments, examinations and qualifications.

www.surestart.gov.uk
Sure Start is the UK government programme to deliver the best start in life for every child, bringing together early education, childcare, health and family support.

Author Index

Subject Index